STINKER'S NINE LIVES

STINKER'S NINE LIVES

From Dunkirk to D-Day and Beyond

Clive Kemp

Edited and with Introductions by Chris Stone

Foreword by General Sir John McColl,
Lieutenant-Governor of Jersey

SEEKER PUBLISHING

Published in 2013 by
Seeker Publishing
Units 1 & 2 Elms Farm
La Mare Vineyards
La Route De La Hougue Mauger
St Mary
Jersey
JE3 3BA

www.seekerpublishing.com

Origination by Seaflower Books
www.ex-librisbooks.co.uk

Printed by CPI Anthony Rowe
Chippenham, Wiltshire

© 2013 Seeker Publishing

ISBN 978-0-9927159-0-8

Seeker
Publishing & Distribution
in the Channel Islands

To all my fallen friends

Contents

Simon Crowcroft wrote this poem following a trip to the Normandy landing beaches. Entitled 'En route to Pegasus Bridge', it is dedicated to Clive Kemp, President of the Jersey Normandy Veterans Association:

En route to Pegasus Bridge

Pass in comfort over drowned meadows,
doomed intersections, the fatal hill;
nothing remains, yet from the windows
glimpses tease your memory; the spill
of hay from broken barns, the hedgerows
thick with may, the spire at Bénouville.

Plant the wooden cross in Dransfield's grave,
who took your place in the turret, and
bullets meant for you. Bless him who gave
long nights and days by the ten thousand,
and asked for nothing in return, save
this 'Thank you', in a spidery hand.

FOREWORD

by

General Sir John McColl
The Lieutenant-Governor of Jersey KCB, CBE, DSO

Many accounts of the Second World War portray the political and strategic decisions that shaped the course of history from the perspective of politicians and commanders. There are very few accounts that answer the question that most of us want answered: 'What was it really like for those fighting on the ground in the front line?'

In this graphic and detailed account Sapper Clive Kemp, with the help of Chris Stone of the BBC, describes the uncertainty, loneliness, camaraderie, chaos, tragedy, loyalty and humour of war.

Clive Kemp signed up at South Hill in 1940, aged just nineteen, and was discharged at the end of hostilities aged twenty-five. In the intervening years he experienced Dunkirk, the Blitz, the Normandy landings, Pegasus Bridge, the freedom of Anderlecht and Brussels, and the final push across the Elbe. To have survived one of these operations would be remarkable, but to have lived through them all is quite extraordinary.

This dramatic story is told in straightforward, matter-of-fact language which makes it all the more compelling. Clive Kemp's impressive array of medals, which includes the *Légion d'honneur*, bears witness to his progress across Europe in the forward elements of the advancing Allied army. In doing so he contributed directly to the freedom of his island home.

This is a story of a young Jersey man's service and sacrifice during a traumatic period and I commend it to all who try to understand the reality of war in the twentieth century.

ACKNOWLEDGEMENTS

I would like to thank Chris Stone for his time and dedication in getting my story told.

Chris would like to thank Caroline for her patience and Mary for the endless supply of tea and cake.

The publishers would like to thank Vicky Aldus for proofreading, Roger Jones for origination and Clive Kemp, the Imperial War Museum and the *Jersey Evening Post* for permission to reproduce the images in this book.

Front and back cover images courtesy of the Imperial War Museum and Clive Kemp.

About Chris Stone

Chris Stone is a BBC journalist and broadcaster who has lived in Jersey for more than twenty years. He has made many radio documentaries about the experiences of islanders who were held there during the German Occupation, and those who fought so that it could be freed. He continues to regard them as heroes, even if they protest otherwise.

INTRODUCTION

by

Chris Stone

Every man thinks meanly of himself for not having been a soldier.
Samuel Johnson

I first met Clive when, as a BBC reporter, I was sent to the cinema to watch *Saving Private Ryan*. The film, in which Tom Hanks and his American buddies win the Second World War, was perhaps the first to show the invasion of Normandy on D-Day as it truly was for the average soldier: terrifying, noisy, and often confusing. Members of the newly formed Jersey branch of the Normandy Veterans Association had been invited to watch the film, and my brief was to ask them what they thought of it afterwards.

It was an assignment which I was looking forward to. The experience of people at war has fascinated me for as long as I can remember. I was brought up in Plymouth, an important naval base still, and a prime target for German bombers during the war. My grandparents were bombed out of their home twice. Their last home, which I remember clearly, had an ominous-looking, ivy-covered shelter in the back garden. Outside in the road was a siren which sounded regularly to signal the end of shifts at the nearby dockyard. A few short decades before, its wail had signalled the nightly onslaught of the Blitz.

My bookshelves as I grew up were filled with books about the conflict. *The Great Escape, A Bridge Too Far*, illustrated histories, *The World at War* on television, all fascinated me. *The World at War* in particular was enthralling because people who had actually been in the thick of it were there, on my television screen, telling me what it had been like.

So here, on this work assignment, was my chance to meet some of these men whose exploits I had learned so much about. What they had in common was that they had served, in some way, in Normandy in the summer of 1944, many of them on D-Day itself. They were soldiers, sailors and airmen who had taken part in perhaps the greatest invasion in history.

So what did I expect when I met them?

Frankly, I expected heroes. After all, some of them had been dropped as Paras on Pegasus Bridge, landed with the Commandos at Juno Beach, flown bombing missions over enemy territory, fired broadsides from battleships. They would, in my eyes, have every right to swagger their way around, swathed in medals and basking in adulation from a grateful nation.

Of course they did nothing of the kind. None of them looked or acted in any way like a hero. They were gentlemen: polite and considerate, smartly dressed, any one of whom you would walk past in the street without giving a second glance. Some were ready to tell me there and then what they thought of the film; most said the battle scenes were very realistic, although they had the expected British serviceman's gripe that the bloody Yanks were trying to say they won the war! Others found it painful to talk about, and told me that they had tried not to think about what had happened to them, and had never told their story. With many of them came the moment, which I have seen in many veterans and survivors of conflicts since, when they feel they have told you enough. Their eyes lose their focus, they look away into the distance, and it is as though a curtain comes down. The memories are just too painful to recall. For many of them that night, it was the first time someone of my generation had asked them just what they had been through. I found that both unbelievable and terribly sad.

After that evening I wanted to hear more. I became an associate member of the Veterans Association, and went to many of their dinners. I would regularly find myself sharing a glass of wine with men who, in that summer of 1944, had been some of the fittest, fiercest and finest young men in the world. Now in their eighties and nineties, they had found a comradeship and a chance to talk about what they had done. In recent years, they have had a ceremony at the cenotaph in St Helier on 6 June. Clive reads the Kohima Epitaph. He rarely gets through it without choking, as the memories come flooding back in those few simple words.

I was lucky enough to go to Normandy with the veterans for the sixtieth anniversary of the D-Day landings. Squeezed into one of seemingly hundreds of similar coaches, we toured the battlefields, beaches and cemeteries. The heads of nations applauded as these proud men marched by. It was an incredibly moving trip, and I felt privileged to be there. I made a documentary about the experience, with many veterans sharing their thoughts and recollections. Searching for a title, I kept coming back to what one of them had said. This grey-haired old man, chest covered in medals and surrounded at Pegasus Bridge by people wanting to take his photograph, told me that he and his mates were nothing special. He didn't really understand all the fuss. 'After all,' he said, 'we were just ordinary fellows.' *Ordinary Fellows* immediately became my title, and for me it epitomises the modesty I have found in all of these men.

The man who gave me that phrase was Clive. He was a bundle of energy, a slight, still-agile man who took on a lot of the administrative duties of the Association. He was happy to talk about his experiences, but he always downplayed his part. He also had a wicked sense of humour, always ready for a laugh, especially at the expense of anyone in authority. It was only as I got to know him better over the next few years that I realised just what a unique individual he was. Not only had he lied about his age to join up and leave Jersey on the eve of its occupation, but he had also been part of the ill-fated British Expeditionary Force, and been taken off the Mole at Dunkirk. He had dug up unexploded bombs in London during the Blitz. He had landed on D-Day, been based at Pegasus Bridge, seen the battle of the Falaise Gap, been a part of the forces of Operation Market Garden, bridged the Rhine, and helped to rebuild a shattered and defeated Germany. I never tired of asking him about his memories.

Then one day he phoned me up, and asked if I would help him to put it all down on record. He was older now, and had difficulty walking. He wanted to have an account of his life which he could pass on to his grandchildren. So began eighteen months of weekly meetings at his house, when he would delve back into a lifetime of memories for my listening voice recorder. We laughed, cried and drank tea together. His patient wife Mary kept us well-supplied with her home-made cake. Eventually, with the recordings finished, I began to write down what he had told me, in his own words, so that his family could hear his voice through the page.

When it was nearly done, he asked me one day if I thought anyone else might be interested in hearing what he had to tell. Having spent most of his life in silence about the war, he wasn't convinced that they would be. I am very grateful to Simon Watkins, our publisher, for coming to Clive's house with me to persuade him otherwise.

It has been a pleasure and a privilege to help Clive to tell his story. There were thousands of 'ordinary fellows' like him, to whom my generation owes an enormous debt. The words I have written here can only go a very short way in describing this kind, humble, fun-loving man; I will let his words speak for him. I am proud to call him my friend.

In this modern age, the word 'hero' is overused. But sometimes, I believe, it is very well-deserved. Clive, of course, would disagree ...

Chapter One

GROWING UP

On Wednesday, 20 October 1920, Benest's auctioneers were proud to announce on the front page of *Les Chroniques de Jersey* newspaper that the business was to be developed considerably. The island's French language broadsheet was pleased to inform readers that Mr Benest's four sons had just been demobbed from HM Forces, and they were able to help their father create a Country Department. It would specialise in cattle, farms, effects, crops and furniture.

This advertisement captures in a few lines the Jersey of Clive's birth. The small island, nine miles by five, tucked into the crook of France between Brittany and the Cherbourg Peninsula, was very different to the island we know today. There was no multi-billion pound finance industry to keep it wealthy, and tourism was still in its infancy. Agriculture was everything, and the newspapers make that clear. *Les Chroniques*, and the English language *Evening Post*, are almost entirely filled with advertisements concerning farming.

The famous Jersey cow dominated; you were informed that Mytilda's Beau, a bull which was the offspring of prize-winning animals General Service and Mytilda's Belle, was available to service any cow which local farmers cared to bring to his bovine boudoir at Les Niemes in St Peter. The cost would be ten shillings.

Farmers were advised that they could buy the best quality

army boots at F. Ching's Boot Stores at number 23 Broad Street. The *Post* announced that tomatoes were fetching between eight and twenty shillings per cental (a hundredweight, or about forty-five kilos) at the Weighbridge, and that Mister J. A. Maurice would be threshing in his land at Bel Royal to finish the season.

Many of the people working the land would have been men who had gone away to fight for their country. Hundreds either joined The Jersey Company, a unit which fought with distinction in the Royal Irish Rifles on the Somme and at Passchendaele, or were sent individually to other units. Jersey has a proud tradition of fighting for its own independence – and for the Crown which allowed it that right. In 1781 the Jersey Militia, led by Major Francis Peirson, had routed a French force which had invaded the island intent on occupation. Their descendants had turned out to fight for the country in the Great War, at the cost of many dead. It had been over for barely two years.

But times were not always easy for the returned heroes of the conflict; especially not on the mainland. In the few column inches of the island newspapers not dwelling on cattle, tomatoes and land sales, several articles lament the main national story of the day: the miners' strike. Thousands of men, many of them former soldiers, had downed their tools, left the pits and demanded a pay rise of two shillings a day. The matter was far from resolved, and its effects were felt in the island too. Notices informed people that the mail steamer would only sail once the following week, and that people should be economical in their consumption of coal. It even meant less sugar for everyone; because of transport problems due to the strike, the sugar ration was reduced to six ounces per person per week.

Those who lamented the hardship of going without coal, sugar and mail, may have missed two of the other stories of the day.

The Suffragette Miss Sylvia Pankhurst had been arrested in England for making 'seditious statements' in a newspaper. Universal suffrage was still eight years away. And an article from Central News revealed that discussions were well under way to arrange for an Unknown Soldier to be laid to rest in Westminster Abbey on Armistice Day, the following month.

Meanwhile, at a rather posh club in St Helier, the club steward was becoming a father for the fifth time ...

I was born on 20 October 1920, in the United Club in Jersey's Royal Square. My father Percy was the head steward there. He had arrived in Jersey with a battalion of soldiers which had been sent to the island; he was originally from Hampshire. My mother was Jersey through and through.

I was child number five, and my so-called parents only kept the first three. My sister, born before me, was sent out to foster care to an old lady. I was sent off to live with an aunt for the first two years of my life. I can't even remember what she looked like.

I'm told I always looked snotty and dirty when I was very young, and was allowed to run around wherever I pleased; and really, that's how my life began. At the age of two I used to play around the Cheapside area. There was this man who was a lamplighter for the Jersey Gas Company, and whenever he saw me he'd always take me to Freeman's Bakery for a cake. Then one day he found me with bloody knees from falling over, and he asked me where I lived. So I told him, and he took me up the road to see this aunt of mine.

He said, 'I keep seeing this little lad wandering round, and I buy him a bun ... My wife and I can't have children and we see this happening!' So she said, 'Look Mr Osborne, if you go down the Square and ask for Percy Kemp at the club, I'm sure he'll be glad to let you adopt this child.'

So my dad went down there that same evening with my mother – and whenever I say 'mum' or 'dad' now, I mean my adoptive parents – they went to the club that same evening, and Percy Kemp said, 'Yes, we're quite happy for you to have him, we'll pay you two and six a week.'

Well the money came in for the first few months and then it stopped. Now, my dad was as poor as a church mouse – he was a labourer at the gasworks. So he went down to the club and said, 'Look, you've stopped paying!' and Percy Kemp said, 'Ah well, bring him back, I'm sure somebody else'll take him.'

Now look at that picture of me, at two years old; now, is anybody going to say 'Right, take him back'? Especially as they wanted children.

So I think my father must have said, 'You stick your bloody half-crown, we'll keep him!' And from then on he never had any money for me.

Now about four years after that my mother became pregnant. She had a daughter, and two years after that she had a son; but I was always their favourite, as their firstborn. And they treated me very well, as one of their own, and I got everything that their own children had.

We lived in Philips Street, close to the gasworks, in a small two-bedroomed place near where the Arts Centre is now.

It was very basic, all gas lighting, with a toilet in the garden. You had to come down with a candle in the middle of the night, and a bucket from the pump. It was rough in those days; one job we used to have to do in the evenings was cut up the newspaper into squares, and tie a bit of twine though it; that was for the toilet. The toilet

Cute, wasn't I?

had a space above and below the door, and when you were sitting there the wind would whistle through and blow out the candle! We lived there for about three years, and then moved across to Tunnel Street, to a place that was owned by the gasworks. We shared a communal garden with other families, and it was really good living. We were poor, but we were happy. I was a bit of tearaway. I always used to tease my mother, squeezing her arms as she went past me to make her chase me. There were ten or twelve stairs down from our house and I used to jump the

19

bloody lot, and of course she didn't follow me then! It was all done for fun.

I used to sleep in the attic with my younger brother, and I was always the fussy one. My clothes had to be packed away before I went to bed but we didn't have a wardrobe. So I made one, and my mum gave me an old curtain that went round it. My brother, on the other hand, was a scruffy little bugger, and he was always being told off for not being tidy like me!

Dad used to help me look smart. Down by where Minden Place car park is now, there used to be a cattle market, and next to it there was a little market where they used to sell things like clothes and bits and bobs. A Mr Green used to sell suits. One time my dad said that I needed a new suit. So down we went to see this Mr Green and we chose one. When we got it home though, the trousers turned out to be knickerbockers, which I really didn't want.

'I'm not bloody wearing that!' I said.

'Yes you are, it cost me money!'

'No I'm not! They're really old fashioned, people play golf in them!' Eventually he got them cut at the tailors to make them fit properly. The jacket was single-breasted, but far too long for me; it hung down almost to my knees. I hardly ever wore it.

There were three boys living next door, and they used to take me to school at St Luke's. I was an average kid, but I liked girls more than I liked school. It was a mixed school. I was always liked by the teachers because I was always polite and clean. But I was always in trouble for doing things I shouldn't – mostly having a go at girls, pulling their skirts as they passed and things like that.

With my adoptive cousin Doreen, aged about three. We ended up as husband and wife!

At playtime there was always a master outside, watching. The playground was divided: girls on one side, boys on the other. One day I went to the toilet, and I was standing there with some of the other blokes and I wondered, 'Can I piss over the wall?' So I had a go, and *pssst*! over the wall it went. And the bloody teacher was standing on the other side! So I came out, and he asked, 'Who squirted that water over the wall?'

'I did sir!' I replied.

So he sent me to Laurent in Queen Street, where Next is now. He said, 'Get me sixpenny-worth of cane.' The girl at the shop asked what it was for and I told her it was for caning bad boys. She laughed, and gave me the piece of cane. I cycled back to school with it, where the master who had sent me said, 'Right, you're the first one to get a taste of this. I'm going to give you six!' Now they usually want to hit the palm of your hand, and they expect you to pull your hand back a bit so they aim for your wrist. But I didn't move my hand so he caught me right there, and left a weal. I got back home and my dad said, 'What's that?'

So I told him, 'I've had the cane Dad.'

'What for?' he asked.

So I told him it was for pissing over the wall. And my dad laughed, and said, 'You shouldn't do things like that!'

In later life that teacher was the president of the Saturday Football League, and I became the secretary. It was the biggest league in the Channel Islands.

I got into other trouble too, but nothing serious. In those days they used to carry tomatoes and potatoes through town using a horse and cart. So when we were coming back from school these carts were trotting up Don Road. So we'd be trotting behind, we'd grab hold and take as many tomatoes as we could. You'd be filling your pockets, and the farmer would crack his bloody whip to get us off! Potatoes weren't so easy because they were in barrels, but when the cart got jogged about they would fall out and we could grab them.

When I was about eleven or twelve, Mum and Dad thought I was old enough to venture out a bit further. Me and a couple of mates used to go down to the harbour sometimes, fishing with hand lines (we didn't have fishing rods). To make our way home we used to go up South Hill and through the Long Road, behind Fort Regent. Now this was the haunt of a couple of 'ladies of ill repute', and the men off the boats used to meet them and do their bit there. I think they were called French Annie and Lulu Simmonds. Well, we used to run down the Long Road calling them all sorts of names and of course they were always drunk and could never catch us!

Some years later when I was a gas fitter I was sent to one of these houses to do a repair. When the woman opened the door she recognised me right away, and playfully whacked me across the earhole! But she was nice and said let bygones be bygones; we even had a cup of tea together. Nothing else mind you! In those days there were a lot of characters who we used to cheek and then run for it.

I remember my dad used to take me down to the harbour where a yacht called the *Westward* was kept. And we used to fish over the wall there, for flatfish. We spent many a Saturday afternoon catching our tea there. He always encouraged me when I got something: 'Oh, that's a bloody good one Son!'

We both had bikes, and we used to cycle round all the parishes where there were football games. I never missed out on anything. I can still picture him coming home on a Saturday morning, saying, 'Right, Son. Shall we go down to the harbour for a bit of fishing? Or do you fancy heading down to FB Fields for the football?' He would always give me the choice, and always give up his Saturday afternoon for me, and if I'd been out he'd always wait up for me.

They were lovely parents. I used to do jobs for them, like running to the butcher's to buy some back fat to put in the beans, or fetching chips and faggots in a big basin for our tea. Mum used to make bean crock in a big pot, and cover the top with brown paper with 'Osborne' written on it. I'd take it to the baker's on Saturday night for cooking, and pick it up again on the Sunday. I was happy to do it, they looked after me so I was happy to do those little jobs. I was so lucky to have them; I could never have lived with the Kemps. Of the thirteen of us, ten were fostered. Because I was fostered, not adopted, I kept the name Kemp.

At Christmas my dad always used to say to me, 'Right, you go down to the Square, push the bell and wish your father a Happy Christmas.' So I'd go down there, but I was always worried that he'd try to take me back! I used to say, 'My dad sent me down to wish you a Happy Christmas!' I'm sure that must have hurt him. So anyway, he'd put his hand in his pocket and he used to say, 'I suppose I'll have to give you something?' And I used to say, 'My sister Betty sends hers, and my sister Pam.' So he used to have to give me three half-crowns! And I used to give it to my sisters. And that's all. I never had anything else, until eventually I refused to go.

One day years later I was walking up Bath Street when I saw my biological father talking to another man. He said, 'Oh look here's one of my boys. Hello, Son!'

'Hello Mr Kemp!' I replied, and kept on walking!

Another time I was secretary of the Saturday Football League, and we invited Stanley Matthews over, which was a very big thing. On the day of the match I was showing people to their seats when this so-called father of mine came by and said, 'Hello Son, got a seat for your father?'

'Yes,' I replied, 'he's sitting over there! Sorry, the rest are all booked.' Every chance I had, I got back at him. During the war they were among the Jersey people who were deported to Germany. I didn't even go to his funeral.

I left school at fourteen with no real qualifications. A few of our boys, the brainy ones, went to Victoria College on scholarships. They were the ones who were into books, not sport, and they stuck out like sore thumbs. I was into football, I was into cricket; anything that was outdoors I played. I was always fit as a fiddle.

My dad said he'd ask if I could get a job at the gasworks so I could learn a trade. Well there was nothing else I wanted to do anyway, so I started my apprenticeship in 1934.

Chapter Two

OFF TO WORK

In 1934, the Jersey Gas Company was one of the largest employers of young men in the town of St Helier. It dominated the area known as Gas Place, at the bottom of the hill leading up to St Saviour and Five Oaks. As a boy, Clive had watched the enormous gas storage tank being built on gardens and waste ground that he used to play on, almost next door to his home.

It was a perfect place for young men without many qualifications to learn a trade, and to begin to make a way for themselves in the world. Pictures of the workshop in the 1930s show cheery young apprentices with their sleeves rolled up, working away with their tools, overseen by older, more experienced managers in brown workers' coats.

The hours were long and the wages low, but as a fourteen-year-old lad, it would have been Clive's first taste of independence, his first wage packet and a chance to mingle with older people.

He would have been expected to prove himself in a male-dominated environment, to be responsible and to cope with the demands of figures of authority; he did well, and he soon became skilled at his job.

Clive had always been short for his age, and needed to be able to cope with some teasing from the other men; his time at the Gas Company gave him the ideal opportunity to learn how to stand up for himself. His competitive nature and love of sport meant that he had plenty of chances to show what he was made of. It also taught him that a cheeky grin and a joke could often get him into, or out of, trouble!

For many, the promise of a secure job and a regular wage was all they needed. But Clive was an adventurous young man who wanted more from his life. He wanted to see more places and to meet new people – to escape from his small island home and seek adventure in the world. After serving his apprenticeship he was used to dealing with the rough and tumble of a man's job; the army beckoned as an obvious way out.

But it wouldn't be easy. His father's generation had fought the Great War, and remembered only too well the horrors of battle. While Clive never found out exactly what his father had done during the war, he clearly remembers being warned against getting involved in the next one.

But, as Clive says, when you are young, you think you know best...

My dad came home one day and told me he'd asked them to find me a job at the gasworks. He thought it would be good for me to learn a trade. It was going to be a five-year apprenticeship.

My job was to keep the tools clean, keep the boss's drawer tidy, carry the tool bag and generally do all the dirty jobs.

I was put for a while with an elderly fitter. When I say elderly, I suppose he was about thirty! In those days a thirty-year-old man to a fourteen-year-old boy was bloody old. But I respected him; you had to. I was still quite a tearaway, and with the other lads we used to get up to lots of tricks.

Our workshop had duckboards running all the way around the edge of it because it had a stone floor, and there were lots of mice running around. Sometimes we would be cleaning up and one of the boys would shout, 'Mouse!' So we'd be there with sticks and things chasing them. And we'd catch these bloody mice and put them into one of the little cardboard boxes which were always lying around. We'd poke a hole in the top, and then gas them.

Another trick we played was on a real country boy, from St Ouen. His name was Edgar, and he was twice as big as any of us. We used to come in and start at seven o'clock, when the men used to make their time sheets out and then disappear off for breakfast. So we used to sit around and have a sandwich. Now this bloke used to eat half a two-pound loaf for breakfast. One morning, just after he started eating he had to go to the toilet. We had caught a mouse, and we put it in his sandwich. And do you know, he ate the bloody thing, and didn't notice!

I remember my boss was a Mr Cabot; we always had to call him 'Mister'. When we went to do a job at a house, if there was a lady around, he'd always take his jacket off and roll up his sleeves, so he could flex his muscles for her to see. And while they were admiring him I was always copying him behind his back, which gave them a good laugh at his expense! I loved taking the mickey out of him, and I've carried on doing it to people all my life.

There was another fellow who was a right tearaway, even though he had started five years before me. They put us together, and we went and did the gas fittings for some new estates, Langley Avenue and Langley Park. And the things we got up to! Because I was small, I was the one who used to go under the floors. He'd say, 'You go down there, I'll drill a hole and send the pipe down to you so you can do it up.'

Once I was under the floor, and I heard *tap, tap, tap*, and he'd nailed the trap door shut and buggered off home for lunch!

Me (left) at Jersey Gas just two months before I left the island to go to war
(Image courtesy of the Jersey Evening Post)

Another time we were called to a house out at La Rocque. In the old days they always had a fireplace in the bedroom, and there was a little cupboard next to it. These people wanted a wall bracket, so we had to run a pipe up inside the cupboard and bring it out of the wall. So he knelt down to start making the hole in the cupboard. He said, 'Oi Kempy, pass me the pliers,' so I passed them over to him. Then he shouted, ''Ere you are!' and something flicked right into my face. And it was a used sanitary

27

towel. The woman of the house had obviously changed it in the morning and left it there. I'd never even seen one before! He just laughed his bloody head off!

I got my own back on him a few times though, even though he was bigger than me. One time he chased me around some scaffolding, and he'd taken a plank out from the crosspiece, and I fell right through! Luckily, and I think he knew it, it was right above a big pile of builders' sand, and I was OK.

One of the fun things they used to do in those days was have an annual football match between the gasworks and the police. People would look forward to it for weeks. We had to make our own fun in those days; we didn't have television and things like that. Anyway, the coppers in those days were proper big blokes – you wouldn't mess with them.

I was quite a fit lad, and a good footballer, so they picked me for the gasworks team when I was only about fifteen. The problem was that I was tiny – good for nipping about, but if I got caught, then I was in big trouble! During the game, these great big coppers would just pick me up with one hand and chuck me out of the way! It was a laugh, and the crowd loved it. The match was at Springfield, which was quite a big deal for us then.

Another time, I was down at the harbour with one of my mates, on our bikes. He bet me that I wouldn't ride along the land tie, the big beam of wood which ran along the wall to stop you going over. So I got him to hold me up while I got on my bike, and tried not to look down. The tide was out.

'Are you going to do it?' he asked.

'Yes,' I said, 'Just start me off.'

So off I went, and managed about five yards before I fell off – onto the road side, thank goodness. But just as I was getting up, this great big policeman turned up and asked what the bloody hell we were doing. He knew who I was, because me and my brothers were often getting into little scrapes like this. 'You silly little bugger!' he said, and he clipped me across the ear. Luckily, it never got back to my dad.

I got caught for messing about at the potato barrels too. It was the busy season, and the farm carts were coming down to the harbour all the time, pulled by big horses. They would empty the potatoes into sacks, and the empty barrels would be stacked up, five or six high. Me and my mate would turn up on our bikes, and pull the handle on one of the bottom barrels to make the whole lot fall down. I got a clip when they found me doing that too. I suppose I was a wicked little bugger, although it was only fun, we never went out to break anything or hurt anyone.

Despite all this messing about, I was doing well at work. Although I was meant to do five years of apprenticeship, they gave me an assessment after four and a half, and decided I was good enough to go out on my own, as what they called an 'improver'. I was always one of those workers whose job had to look immaculate: if it wasn't I'd do it again.

I had a bit more money to spend now; about fourteen shillings a week. Ten went to my parents, so I had two to spend and two to save.

My friend Chick and I used to spend a lot of time together. He'd joined the company a week before me and lived close by. He eventually married my sister. We tried smoking once. We used to go to town on a Saturday night, chasing the birds. I said to him one day, 'Shall we try smoking a pipe?' You know, we thought we were bloody big. So we went into Woolworths and bought this sixpenny pipe. The tobacconist's was on Mulcaster Street, right opposite the Bunch of Grapes. And there was some tobacco there called cherry cake mixture. So we thought, 'That sounds nice,' and bought half an ounce and a box of matches. We walked up through town and back again, puffing away, thinking we were it. Later that night we were near home, and I said to him, 'I've got terrible guts, Chick,' and so had he. I decided to put my fingers down my throat, and we were both very sick. When we were finished we threw the rest of the tobacco away and broke the pipe. I never smoked again!

I remember the gas company used to organise a day out every year for the workers. Half would go one week, half the next, and I used to try and get on the same one as my dad. That's because my mum asked me to look after him! He never really drank except on these days out, when he'd

29

get a bit tiddly. Everyone had to be at the meeting place in Tunnel Street, where we would get on the charabanc. The stokers were already drunk when they got on, and they used us kids as entertainment. Whenever we got to any stop, they'd get us to race each other for a tanner: 'First one there and back gets one and six!' and that was good money in those days. And they used to make us sing. I can always remember my first song, with my mate Chick. We used to sing 'Don't Fence Me In' as a duet, and the men would throw us pennies and things.

When I couldn't get on the same trip as Dad, Mum used to make us wait for them to come back. I can remember very clearly hearing them coming from the direction of David Place, singing 'Here we are, here we are again'. And Mum would tell us to get out and help my dad. He'd shout, 'Hello Son!' and kiss me, but Mum shouted, 'Bring him over here!' which wasn't easy because he wanted to say goodbye to all the boys. I helped him up Tunnel Street to St Saviours Road where we lived. She would have the couch ready for him in the kitchen, with a blanket and a bucket, and tell him, 'You're not sleeping with me tonight!' I used to make sure he was all right. But the next morning he was always as right as rain, I can't ever remember him being sick.

I got myself a lovely girlfriend too, called Audrey. In those days it was all very well-behaved, although we always used to make sure we headed for the back row when we went to the cinema. We'd sit there and hold hands, sharing a box of chocolates. Afterwards I'd walk her home, and we'd share a bag of chips.

Having said that, I was a bit of a Jack the Lad, and there were lots of other girls I fancied. One of them was the usherette at the cinema! And I remember sitting at the end of the row of seats, holding Audrey's hand in my left hand, in the dark. What she didn't know was that I was holding the usherette's hand with my right!

There was one night I said to Audrey, 'I don't fancy chips tonight, let's just get you home.' It was because I was on a promise with the usherette – I left Audrey and legged it back to the cinema to meet her!

But soon after that the war broke out, and boys that I knew from the gasworks started joining up. I used to talk about it with my mates, in particular the three brothers who lived next door to me – Alf, Reg and Dennis Jourdan. By January 1940 about half a dozen of the older lads had already gone, and we wanted to do our bit. I was still too young. So I said to my dad, 'Alf, Reg and Dennis are thinking of joining up, and I want to go as well.' The first thing he said was, 'I don't want you to.' You must understand, I was a blue-eyed boy, green as hell. My parents used to do everything for me. I never cleaned my own shoes, didn't know how to make a cup of tea, had no sense of the world. My dad knew all about army life because he'd served in India during the First World War. He never spoke much about it, unless he was with other men from the gasworks who had been involved too. The brothers' parents didn't want them to go either.

I think I wanted to go because it seemed exciting, like it would be a big experience for me.

Anyway, at the end of January we had badgered our parents about signing up so much that my dad said, 'Look son, I don't want you to go, but if you want to I won't stop you. You're going to make your bed and you're going to lie in it.'

So one morning the four of us headed up to the registration centre in the gym at South Hill. We all had bicycles, so we rode up there.

There were quite a few lads waiting there, and two of the brothers went in before me. We were all tradesmen, so he must have said that he could get them into the service corps.

They came out, and told us to go in. We were like little kids. There was this great big recruiting officer, sitting behind a wooden table. He was all puffed up, with a red sash across his uniform to show everyone how important he was. He asked us our names: Dennis Jourdan and Clive Kemp. 'Right,' he asked, 'how old are you?' Now, I've always told the truth, so I said I was nineteen in October. This was in January 1940.

Dennis was a similar age. And the recruiting officer said, 'I'm sorry lads, but I can't take you until you're twenty.' And our faces dropped! So we went outside and on the way out we told the other two brothers that we'd come back later and say we were twenty. 'No you won't,' they said, 'You just go and speak to your fathers!'

When my dad came home for lunch, he asked me how we'd got on. I told him they'd refused us. 'Good!' he said!

Anyway, from that Thursday until the Saturday, I kept on and on at him. Eventually he said, 'You're getting on my nerves. If you want to go, go. But you haven't got my blessing.' So I went next door to find Dennis and told him my dad had said I could go; and of course Dennis' dad said, 'Well I can't stop him now, can I?'

So off we went on our bikes, up to South Hill. We sat in the same seats. 'Names?'

'Kemp, Jourdan.'

'How old are you?'

'Twenty, twenty.'

He asked us all the other questions, religion and so on. What worried me was that there was a note at the bottom that said if you made a false declaration there was a fine of five pounds. That was a lot of money in those days. He asked, 'Have you read that?'

'Yes.'

And I can still see the grin on his bloody face.

'Right,' he said, 'You have to sign on for six and six.'

That's six years of service, six years in the reserves. Twelve years of your life! Anyway, he said we'd be in the Engineers, because we were both tradesmen.

'When do you want to go?'

'Monday?'

So he made out the passes for a boat on the Monday, the mail boat.

When it came to it, my dad couldn't say goodbye. He came to the pier, but he was too upset. He went up onto the top wall and waved from there. I can picture him to this day waving his hanky, and it still gives me a lump in my throat.

Chapter Three

TO ENGLAND

Clive had joined up at a time when things were looking bleak for his country. The war was well and truly underway, and by January 1940 the Allies were certainly having the worst of it.

War had been declared on 3 September 1939, just four months before, but since then there had been a series of disasters.

Poland, invaded by both Germany and Russia, had collapsed despite heroic resistance, and surrendered on 27 September. Europe looked to America to help, but President Roosevelt told his people that the United States would take no part in a continental war.

On 14 October 1939, HMS *Royal Oak* was torpedoed in Scapa Flow, with the loss of 833 sailors.

Neville Chamberlain, the man whose piece of paper had promised peace in our time, was still prime minister, although he had appointed Winston Churchill First Lord of the Admiralty.

A major land war in Europe was inevitable, and many looked to France as the next battlefield. The French comforted themselves with the thought that the Maginot Line, a series of linked forts protecting their north-eastern border and built after the First World War using German reparation money, would keep them safe. After all, the Germans would have to go through the apparently impenetrable Ardennes region if they were to invade again ...

Nonetheless, Britain had begun to re-arm, very late in the

day, to prepare for conflict. While Hitler had been building tanks, planes and guns for years, openly flouting the restrictions placed on his country at the end of the First World War, Britain had clung desperately to the hope that peace would prevail. The invasion of Poland had proved that Hitler had no intention of honouring any previous agreements, and was intent on conquering Europe.

For Clive, thrust into the real world of soldiering, the threat of war was less immediate than the need to fit in with his new comrades. The young man, who had spent his life among friends on a small island, was suddenly surrounded by rough-and-ready soldiers with barrack-room language, ready to solve disputes with their fists. He would have to cope with thieves, bullies and army discipline if he was to survive. He'd been sent to join 695 General Construction Company, Royal Engineers, a unit set up to provide all sorts of engineering to the army. He was classed as a plumber because of his experience in the gasworks, although his duties would soon extend far beyond such mundane tasks.

It wasn't a bad crossing; I've always been a good sailor. There were lots of other lads on board too, lots of them had already joined up and were on their way back from embarkation leave. When we docked, either at Southampton or Weymouth, we were put on a train to Chatham. That was the Royal Engineers Depot.

Of course lots of us were just completely green; we'd never been away from home before.

Young men of fighting age leave the islands for England after signing up

We got to the main barracks, called Brompton. For those days, it was quite a modern place. The first thing we had to do, still in our civilian clothes, or civvies, was to get a medical. I got to the right place with my mate, only to find there were two queues to see a doctor and get him to sign you off as fit. One of the queues had about sixty blokes in it, the other only had about twenty, so I said, 'Come on, let's join the small one sharpish!' Anyway, some of the other blokes started sniggering, and we soon found out why. It turns out the doctor we were about to see was a woman. In I went, and the first thing she said was, 'Right, drop your trousers!' and she put a pencil under my willy to check I didn't have anything wrong down there. I couldn't help myself, I was always a bit of a cheeky bugger, I went and gave a bit of a wolf whistle. And I got a right telling off, because she was an officer! Then I had to bend over so she could look up my rectum as well!

Eventually they said, 'Right, we'll kit you out here and give you a bit of drill, but you can't sleep here. There's a barracks down the road which has been condemned; you can sleep there.'

When we got down there it was a real bloody dump. It was like a brick Nissen hut, filthy, with these little pull-out beds, and you had three biscuits to make a mattress; a biscuit was a straw-stuffed palliasse, two inches thick. Two blankets. And there was a box at the end of the bed to put your clothes in. I remember looking at it all and thinking, 'Oh, Christ!'

Anyway, we put our beds out and were told to report for a meal, which was rough, as you can imagine. But because we had travelled we were hungry, and at least it was hot.

Then they warned us that we would be woken up early, and had to get down on to the parade ground sharpish, fully dressed. They gave us some uniforms, all mixed up; they said we'd have to swap things around and maybe make some alterations to make them fit, especially me because I'm so short! The rest of the day we spent just getting to know the barracks, learning how to sign in and out and all that sort of stuff.

When I went to bed that first night there was a crowd there and they were from Manchester. There must have been about fifty or sixty of them and it looked like we were going to join them. They were bloody rough those Manchester boys – well, they were men really, all from the same firm, and they had joined the Engineers because of their skills. The day had been so rough that I cried myself to sleep. I did it again the second night, but eventually I toughened up and started to give as good as I got.

The first morning there I woke up and wanted to pack my clothes neatly in the box at the end of the bed. And someone had taken my bloody box!

The second day my cap badge was missing and I asked if anyone could help me. One of the blokes said, 'Yeah, I can sell you one.' And of course it was my own bloody badge which I had to buy back off him.

I managed to get on with them eventually, even though one of my early mates got moved. I became friends with a bloke called Rice, who was a bit of a wide boy. He had all sorts of tricks that I'd never even heard of.

Sometimes we'd get a weekend pass, and he'd always want to go home. He'd ask, 'Why don't you come home with me?' but I never had any money. He said, 'Don't worry about the money, I can get you on the train!'

So we got to the railway station and he asked for two returns to the next station, which was from Chatham to Gillingham. But as soon as we were outside, he licked all the ink off the tickets and wrote Manchester on them instead! And he was full of tricks like that. I had to fall in with their ways in the end, I had to. It was either beat them or join them, so I joined them! And if truth be told, I enjoyed it, taking chances and having a lot of fun.

One evening I had a night off, and so I decided to go to

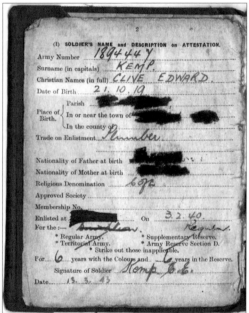

My army pay book: note my wrong date of birth after I had to lie to get signed up

the cinema. I remember it was a Laurel and Hardy film, and I always liked them. Anyway, I found a seat in the dark, and started to enjoy myself. There was a really funny bit and the bloke next to me started laughing, a real loud laugh. And I thought to myself, 'I recognise that laugh.' It was my mate Chick McGrath from Jersey! He'd come over a week before me. There were six cinemas he could have gone to in Chatham, and hundreds of seats, and he ended up sat next to me! We had a right laugh about that.

We went out for a drink afterwards, and found ourselves a nice couple of birds. I remember it was raining, so we snuggled them into a doorway while we stayed out in the rain. We were enjoying their company when I felt a hard tap on my shoulder. I heard a nasty voice saying, 'Soldier, are your hands cold?'

'No, why?' I asked.

'Then get them out of your f***in' pockets!'

It was a redcap, a military policeman, whose job it was to keep discipline. Talk about embarrassed!

We were good at being soldiers though, we did what we had to do. Having said that, I do remember none of us wanted to carry our gas masks around, they were in a cardboard box that you had to sling around your neck. So we always dumped them in a hedge near barracks when we went anywhere, and picked them up afterwards.

There was about a fortnight at Chatham, learning the basics. Drill took ages, being shouted at: 'Left turn, right turn, about turn!' and they were always yelling because people were turning the wrong way and making a mess of it all the time. We had a right laugh.

We had to go to courses, listening to them explain to us what we'd have to do as Engineers. Lifting mines, fixing roads and things like that; there was never any talk of bridges in those days.

It was in Chatham that I had my first tattoo done on my arm, as soon as I could after joining the army. I wanted to have 'Death or Glory', but eventually I settled for 'True Love', with the name of the bird I was seeing in Jersey. Of course over the years I had to have it over-written a couple of times. Now, all these years later, it's just a blur.

Then I had to go on a trade course to show that I was up to standard with my fitting job. The tasks they gave me I could have done standing on my head. Making joints in those days was simple. You had a blowlamp to heat it up, and I could do it easily.

We moved from Chatham to Margate, and there was a big entertainment complex there, called Dreamland. And there were a lot of Polish Air Force men there, and my lot would always start fights with them. But because I was small I would always stay out of the way! Because of that, and the fact that I was younger than the rest of them and quite quick, they always called me Nipper, never Clive. Anyway, I was always more interested in girls than fighting, so I'd always head out looking for girls instead of going to get drunk with the rest of them. In those days it was just platonic ... most of the time! I had the gift of the gab, a silver tongue, and I worked out just how to get sympathy. 'I'm from Jersey, a long way from my mum and dad, feeling lonely...' and they would always say, 'Oh, come home and have tea with me!' and that's how I really got on. Often we'd meet them at the local roller-skating rink.

At Margate they really started to toughen us up. We were billeted in hotels right along the sea front. They had evacuated the area, so we had it all to ourselves. Each morning we had to march to a hall for breakfast, then it would be, 'Right, fall in! We're going on a twenty-mile march!' – what they'd call a forced march. The first one I did, oh! I'd been a spoiled boy at home, always in nice shoes. Here they gave us hobnail boots, which were bloody heavy. Then off we'd go, quick march, three abreast with full pack. We didn't have rifles because there weren't enough of them to go round. And they marched us for twenty miles without stopping. When we stopped, I think near Ramsgate, I undid my boots, just like the rest of them. 'Christ,' we said, 'I hope there's not too much more of this!' And then of course after a half-hour rest I couldn't get the bloody things on again! I had to tie my laces together, put the boots around my neck, and walk the rest of the way just in my socks! My feet started bleeding. When we got back to Margate they shouted, 'Halt! Right, now you're going for your swimming test! Keep all your gear on, and get into the pool!'

'Christ,' I thought, 'I can't bloody swim!'

We went inside to where they had this great big swimming pool, and I had to think quickly, although I was scared as hell. So I went up to the sergeant, and said I was busting to use the toilet. 'Right, quick!' he said. I waited inside the toilet, looking out through the doorway to see what was happening; I realised that they were only making us swim widths. So I came back out and joined the queue of blokes at the shallow end. And that was how I passed my swimming test, hopping from foot to foot across the pool.

Back we went to the hotel. We had some food there, and got straight to bed. The problem was, we had nowhere to dry our heavy khaki uniform, so the next morning it was still soaking. These days you'd be worried about catching pneumonia!

Then they took us to the beach and made us march through the sand. And with the wet and the sweat, the grit just stuck to you and was bloody uncomfortable. Actually, I was given some extra sand marching to do, for a reason.

There were some visitors there, watching us being marched to and fro. And they started booing the sergeants, telling them to leave us alone and stop being so horrible. I shouted back to them, 'Yes, the bastards!' And of course the sergeant heard, and said, 'Right Kemp, you get an extra half-hour!'

This sergeant took a dislike to me. He had a little moustache like Errol Flynn, which made me laugh. Every time we had to 'number off', one, two, three; when it came to me I'd say my number with a smirk. And one day he said to me, 'I'll take that bloody smirk off your face Kemp!' and that was me down for an extra hour's sand marching. It was my own fault; I was always a bit saucy to them. I wasn't disrespectful, just cheeky or witty, and it got me into trouble.

Some relatives of mine sent me some pictures of Margate recently.

The old hotel where we were billeted is now a centre for immigrants. The place hasn't changed much.

Once we'd been toughened up at Margate we were ready to do our job, so we were sent on embarkation leave. Most of the lads went to Manchester; I went back to Jersey.

*Me with my mum at the harbour while back
in Jersey on embarkation leave, 1940*

41

Chapter Four

ESCAPE FROM DUNKIRK

Clive was to be part of the British Expeditionary Force (BEF), the second such force to be sent to France in the twentieth century. The first, sent to defend against the German invasion of 1914, had managed to stem the enemy advance at the battle of Mons with its discipline and accurate shooting.

The one mustered at the end of 1938 was to have no such luck. The first group, of 158,000 men, was sent across in October 1939, after the beginning of the war and the occupation of Poland. It was poorly-equipped in comparison to the well-prepared German army, which had already honed its blitzkrieg tactics against the Poles.

695 General Construction Company, Royal Engineers, would join the British force later, to help with essential engineering tasks such as repairing roads and building airstrips.

They were deployed along the border with Belgium, a neutral country, on the assumption that they would have time to react if the Germans invaded. They were woefully badly-equipped. Although the factories at home were now working flat out, the shortage of basics such as rifles and even bullets was shocking for an army which was preparing to take on the *Wehrmacht*. While more men, including Clive, arrived, they didn't bring with them the supplies they so badly needed. By the time the Germans arrived there were nearly 320,000 men of the BEF waiting for them, as well as the French divisions manning the Maginot line and other defences.

They would never be enough. Hitler's army and air force were already toughened by their actions in Poland and had perfected the art of blitzkrieg, or lightning war. That meant soldiers could move forward quickly, supported by tanks and close aerial bombardment.

After the long wait of the so-called Phoney War, when the soldiers in France and the population back home wondered what was happening, Hitler's invasion of Western Europe began. Troops swept through neutral Belgium, bypassed the Maginot Line by pushing through the Ardennes, and threatened to trap British and French forces by cutting them off from the south, leaving them nowhere to go but the sea.

Clive and his comrades, with just seventy-five days of training, few bullets and little air support, were almost defenceless. Together with virtually the whole of the BEF, they retreated through crowds of refugees, under constant attack from the air, to a small port in the north of France: Dunkirk. As the German noose drew tighter, the British Army abandoned what equipment it had left in the dash for safety. The Germans captured prisoners by the hundreds, sweeping all before them.

Eventually, the survivors of 695 General Construction Company made it to the dunes at De Panne, at the eastern end of the Dunkirk beaches. What greeted them was a terrible sight. The beach was full of men, lining up to try to get away to one of the boats moored off the coast. They were attacked by aircraft and shellfire, and there were injured men and bodies strewn among the wreckage of lorries, trucks and guns.

As engineers, they eventually found themselves working to repair the Mole, a long wooden causeway which, after the docks were bombed, became the only place where big ships could tie up to take on soldiers. The work was constant, and dangerous, as the Germans were well aware that it was an important escape route. Eventually they got their turn to get away – in one of the last ships to leave. Clive believes that it was identical to the old Jersey mailboat which he regularly used to see tied up in St Helier harbour.

The evacuation was complete, and Churchill was able to claim it as a victory. More than 300,000 men had come off the beaches at Dunkirk, to form the basis of a new army to protect the country.

They had escaped the fate of many of their comrades, who were left behind injured, dead, or as prisoners.

For Clive, a young man from Jersey, there was death and destruction he could never have imagined. He lost friends and buried enemies. It was a baptism of fire that would leave him deeply shocked, and with memories which still make him cry today.

My mum met me off the boat from England, because my dad was working. I've still got a photo of that moment. I carried my civilian clothes, and of course I was dressed up in my uniform. Kidding myself, as usual!

When I'd left the island to join the army I'd had a girlfriend. To be honest I was getting a bit fed up with her; she was quite a bossy young lady, and when I went to see her things weren't really any better. I don't think she liked me being in the army.

But we kept writing, and eventually she finished it while I was away during the war. She met and married some other bloke, but I wasn't really upset because I'd been meeting lots of other girls anyway.

Mum and Dad were really proud of me if I'm honest, and they went around showing me off. Even my dad was pleased for me, he could see I was happy.

The atmosphere in Jersey was one of anticipation. People knew there was a war coming, and they were ready to fight for their country. But they certainly weren't expecting to be invaded, for German soldiers to be there. Naturally I swanked around town, thinking I was the cat's whiskers. Often people would recognise me in the street, they would stop me and wish me luck. I went into the gasworks to see my mates. The manager heard that I was down in the workshops, and he sent for me. In those days, the manager was called Mr Pepin, and I was Kemp. He made a big fuss of me, called me Clive and shook my hand to wish me luck. That was a big thing. I remember there was a certain café in the market where all the blokes used to go. So I went there to say goodbye to them, but also to show off my uniform!

Of course I never went back to see my biological parents, they were out of my life by then.

Again, when I left Jersey to go back to the mainland, my mum came with me right as far as the boat, but my dad couldn't. He was too choked up. I can still see him clearly, standing at the end of the harbour waving his white handkerchief again, as we went around Elizabeth Castle and out of sight.

We got back to our barracks and within a week we were sent down to Southampton to get on the boat for France.

It was a vessel which had been adapted to carry troops, and it was absolutely full. I was on there with the lot from Manchester, as a construction group. Luckily I don't get seasick because I remember it was quite a rough crossing.

So there I was, after being in the army for just seventy-five days, on my way to France. I had turned from a spoilt Jersey boy into a man. I could hold my own with any of them. When it came down to it we were mates and would look after each other. I came ashore at Le Havre with my best mate Ernie Rice, and we were put into cattle trucks. There was even straw on the floor.

It was while we were there that I first heard that the Germans had taken Jersey. They used to put up a map covered in little flags to show where we were, and where the Jerries were. One day our major called me over and said, 'Kemp, I don't know if you knew about it, but the Germans have landed in Jersey and Guernsey. How do you feel about that?' Of course my parents were there, and I'd had no news from them. I said I hoped I'd hear from them soon, but I didn't really know what else to say.

We were sent up to the north of France, somewhere between Arras and Lens. It's a coalmining area. We were sent there to build emergency landing strips for our fighters, so they didn't have to fly all the way back to England to re-arm and refuel. But before they were finished the Jerries broke through in Holland and Belgium, and were on their way through France heading towards us! Now believe it or not, we had been sent there without a single rifle between five hundred of us! England simply didn't have them.

Eventually a big Army Service Corps lorry pulled up into our camp. A sergeant jumped out and dropped the tailboard down. And he said, 'Right, gather round men. Have any of you used a rifle?'

Well of course I put my hand up. I never had, except for a few goes at the funfair, but I always volunteered for everything. So he threw this bloody rifle at me and it nearly knocked me over! And I had just one clip for it. Five bloody bullets to keep the Germans back! I didn't even know how to load the thing. I was trying to work it out in my tent, pushing the clip in and playing with the trigger and I clearly remember the other blokes shouting, 'For Christ's sake take that outside, or you'll shoot some bugger!'

We finally worked it out, but we had just five rounds of ammunition, and the Germans were coming.

We were building this emergency landing strip, using ash or unwanted coal. We were on eight-hour shifts, with the work going on all day and night. We didn't have very good lights to work with, just acetylene flares. I remember being on from ten at night until six in the morning. It was bloody hard work, a real rush job. At six the whistle used to go, and you would swap with the next lot.

There was one occasion I will never forget. After finishing I wandered back to the camp, which was about a quarter of a mile away. I was thinking about breakfast. But before that, I thought I'd go to the toilet. The toilet was just a hole, about fifteen feet long, and six or seven feet wide. It was about four feet deep, with a screen around it which the carpenters had knocked up. They had also put some logs across it for us to sit on; they hadn't even taken the bark off, so it wasn't very comfortable!

So this particular morning I was sitting there; and because I'm such a short-arse I had to sit in the middle so there was a bit of give in the branches and I could touch the ground.

Then all of a sudden a German plane came down, *brrrrtttt*! strafing the workers nearby. Now I was half asleep after a long night shift, and I jumped out of my skin with fright; I fell right back into the bloody hole, right in the shit! We'd been in that camp for about ten days, and each day all the men would use it and then it would get covered with lime. Can you imagine the sound I made? It was like smacking a jelly. The other blokes saw and heard what happened, and started laughing their bloody heads off! I climbed out, and I was covered in it. No one would help me, they were too busy laughing, and I was calling them all sorts of names back.

I had to get clean, but that wasn't easy. For a tent of eight men, we were allowed a tin of water about eight inches round and eighteen inches high to wash in. But they wouldn't let me near that, so I just walked until I found a little stream. It was very cold, in fact there had been snow around. But I had to strip off my denims, trousers and jacket, to clean all the shit off myself in the running water. Then I walked the mile and a half back to camp, shivering like hell, still without my breakfast. I went to see the quartermaster sergeant, and said, 'Look Sarge, I fell in the bog and I can't wear these any more.'

'Sling 'em in the bin,' he said, 'and get some more. We'll dock the new ones from your wages.' So I had to pay for my new gear. When I got back to the tent the other lads wouldn't let me in, the smell on me was so bad. From then on they always called me Stinker!

Luckily for me there was a copse nearby with an old bunker from the First War. I cleaned that out and put my blankets and palliasse in there. I was a lone sleeper for a long time. All the other blokes used to move away from me when I went to eat with them, but all in a good spirit which I didn't mind. Eventually, after we were able to get our laundry done, the smell died down.

I remember while we were on that site there used to be two civilians who turned up in the mornings with the English papers from a couple of days before. We were queuing up there one day for our papers when suddenly some gendarmes came along in their grey truck. They started arguing with these two civvies, then one of the gendarmes got out his bloody revolver and shot them both right in front of us! Turned out they were spies, fifth columnists. We didn't really understand what was going on at the time though, they just shot them and dumped them in the truck. It really frightened us to be honest. It made us realise there was a war on.

We carried on working on that site until the order came to evacuate because the Germans were coming. We packed up quickly, and jumped in the trucks to get going. We soon came across the streams of people who were fleeing the Germans, lines and lines of them all the way down the roads. They had to get into the ditches so we could get past.

One thing I'll never forget is having to man the Bren gun, mounted on the top of our truck. As we were driving along we saw a great big black aeroplane flying close to us; it must have been a transport plane. It didn't have any markings on it. The five Bren gunners in our lot thought it was going to drop a load of Jerries on us, so we all fired. It dropped and burst into flames. We only found out later it was a Belgian troop plane, carrying soldiers who were on our side. We knew no different though, the adrenaline was flowing though us. I found that often, during the war. When things are dangerous, when the bullets are flying, you can turn from an angel into a devil. It's a case of survival, that's all it comes down to. You're not fighting for your King or Country, but for survival. I was often very scared. When other planes came down too low, we didn't have time to see if they were ours or theirs, *brrrrtttt*! we let them have it. These things happen so quickly, and you have to be the first to shoot. I don't think we shot down any others though. That Belgian plane should have had some markings on it, but that's the way it was in wartime.

I never felt like a killer, but I had a job to do. Sometimes before we could do our job though, we had to fight, because we were always close to the front. Our job was to get bridges and roads ready for the tanks to follow the infantry closely, but the Jerries weren't always ready to let go of the area.

We pulled back quickly though France. We knew how well-equipped the Germans were, they were throwing everything at us. We weren't really trained for this sort of attack, or for any kind of war. The only ones who were, were the pre-war soldiers, although there weren't many of them. The ones we did see used to throw their weight around and tell us what to do because they thought they had more experience than us.

As we got closer to Dunkirk we saw the wrecks of all the British vehicles that weren't needed any more. Trucks, Bren gun carriers, tanks, they had all been abandoned and set on fire. We had to come back through that.

There was chaos everywhere. We managed to stay together more or less, but a lot of others had given up and been captured.

In fact, on our first day of marching after we left our trucks, we were surrounded by the Germans. They had cut off the route to the coast, ordered us to surrender and to stay in the area. I heard them tell our NCOs that we were '*Kaput*', and would become prisoners of war. We weren't fed or anything, just told our war was over. One of the buggers took my watch. But that night, me and another bloke decided we were going to make a run for it. There weren't lots of Jerries about, just sentries patrolling around. We waited until it was dark, and the sentries were a distance away, then crawled out of the field we were held in. My heart was beating like mad, but when you're nineteen you're braver, aren't you? We crawled for about a quarter of a mile, then stood up and started running like hell. Next thing we knew was, 'Halt, who goes there?'

'British soldiers!' we yelled, and we were safe in our own lines again. Of course the next day the Guards managed to push the Germans back a little and all of our lot were freed again, without having to crawl anywhere!

We found our major, a Canadian, and told him about our escape. 'Bloody good for you!' he said. He was a bit of a mad one, to be honest. He liked the fact that we'd had the guts to do it. I'm a small bloke and I don't like getting into fights, but if I have to I will; I'm quite a gutsy type.

We headed on to Dunkirk. To get to the beach you went down through the little town, then suddenly there were the dunes at De Panne, and all these men were standing waiting. We were right at the back of all the troops waiting on the beach for a ship. We didn't understand what was happening at that point; we thought we were going to get on a boat, go around the coast a bit and then carry on fighting. We stayed there in the dunes for a while. There had been some Gurkhas there, and they had dug little tunnels into the sand to escape from the fighters which were strafing the beaches. We used them too, every time the enemy came over. There were lots of attacks. I remember we hated the RAF at the time, because we never, ever, saw a Spitfire or a Hurricane. I know lots of people thought that the RAF were heroes, but we didn't then, they were nowhere to be seen!

We were scared all the time; not the brave Tommies you read about, just scared blokes. Lines of us waiting to get out, get off the beach and onto a boat. Anyone who wasn't scared was just plain stupid.

There were French soldiers on the beaches too, some of them were pushing onto our boats too. They weren't good soldiers, and sometimes we had fights with them; just like the Americans later.

I remember we were based in a big tall warehouse that had been used to store bananas before the war. We would hear these planes coming over, attacking our troops. It took a direct hit on the top floor, the bomb went through the roof and exploded above us. It shook the whole place. A sergeant major, who'd been a lance corporal before the war, was standing by the door crying his eyes out. And that really scared me, I thought things must be really serious. I thought, 'I'm not having this,' so I jumped out with my Lewis gun and blazed away at them, a whole pan of ammunition. But the sergeant major dragged me back in, because he didn't want them to see us and attack us instead.

We stayed around the beach for a day and a half. Nothing seemed to move. We could see all the little boats coming in, and all the blokes wading out to them; but we also saw a lot of them wading back in again because they couldn't get on. We saw bombs hit the oil tanks, with flames and smoke pouring out over everything.

For a nineteen-year-old it was awful; you didn't know what was coming next. I served my apprenticeship of death there. There were so many bodies, badly hit and mutilated. I cried my eyes out for hours at the sight of it. It was bloody terrible. The looks on the faces of those poor blokes was dreadful, some of them frozen in fright at what was happening to them. I was just a spoilt boy who hadn't really seen anything of the world, and my father's words came back to haunt me. I had made my bed, and now I really was lying in it.

Then our major said, 'We're never going to get onto those boats. I've just found out that they are looking for men to help load the wounded onto ships to take them back to England. It's hot there because they are bombing the docks, but if you want to volunteer, come with me.'

We headed out towards the Mole, a long causeway about ten feet wide and a few hundred yards long. It reminded me of the causeway out to Havre des Pas bathing pool in Jersey, just a bit wider and much longer.

We helped to load four or five ships in the next day and a half. But because of the bombing, the ships eventually had to stop going into the docks because they had been so badly bombed. We ended up repairing bomb damage on the Mole. We used some planks to fix the holes which had been blown in it. Then we helped load casualties on stretchers from there. We finally got into the last ship to sail. We'd loaded lots of wounded, and an officer told us, 'Look, you've done your bit, this is your last chance; get on before it's too late.'

I was so bloody tired, I just lay down on the deck amongst the wounded and fell asleep. I don't even remember the name of the boat. The next thing I knew, someone was kicking me and saying, 'Wake up mate, we're back in England!' I looked up and I could see the white cliffs of Dover. I got off the boat, so tired I couldn't have cared if it had been the *Queen Mary*. They said there was a train coming for us.

We were all filthy dirty; we hadn't had a chance to wash. I was one of the few that didn't have a beard, but only because I was too young.

And I'll never forget a redcap having a go at us while we were waiting – he was yelling at us to clean ourselves up. And one of our officers went up to him and said, 'You've never been out of England, but these boys have been to hell and back.' He really put him in his place, and of course we were laughing like hell.

Members of the Church Army and WRVS were there, with tea and things, and other people came down with drinks and sandwiches and cakes for us. They couldn't do enough for us. The women were kissing us, which of course we didn't mind; we were heroes to them. But to me the heroes were the ones who we left in France. We were just the lucky ones. They say a cat has got nine lives; well I reckon I'd used up more lives than that.

During the war, we often had concerts and singalongs, where we would sing all the popular songs of the time. 'White Cliffs of Dover' was always a very important one for me, after Dunkirk. I always cried when we were singing it, even in a big crowd of blokes. Lots of the biggest ones would be crying too. That one, and 'We'll Meet Again'. When the bombs were falling, and we were in the shit, someone would start singing that, and we would all join in with tears streaming down our faces. We were away from home, we were thinking of the people we loved, and we could have been killed the next minute. Were we going to see them again? I still cry just thinking of those old songs which kept us going.

The train arrived, and we got on. We didn't know where we were going, nobody had a clue. I remember, being so small, getting up onto one of the luggage racks to get out of the way and get some sleep. Eventually they told us we were headed for Scotland.

The evacuation of the British Expeditionary Force across the English Channel from Dunkirk on the French coast was hailed in Britain as an extraordinary achievement and the 'little ships of Dunkirk' swiftly entered the mythology of wartime brave deeds © IWM ART LD 305

British anti-aircraft guns lie abandoned at Dunkirk in 1940 © IWM HU 2286

Men of the Royal Ulster Rifles awaiting evacuation at Bray Dunes – about five miles from Dunkirk © IWM HU 1137

Evacuated troops on a destroyer about to berth at Dover © IWM H 1637

Exhausted British troops rest on the quayside at Dover © IWM H 1643

A member of the First Aid Nursing Yeomanry (FANY) serves tea and sandwiches to evacuated troops aboard a train at Addison Road station, London. One of the soldiers is wearing a captured SS German helmet. © IWM H 1635

Chapter Five

AFTER DUNKIRK

Dunkirk had been a dreadful experience. Clive says that his nerves were ruined for a time afterwards – that he couldn't stop shaking and couldn't sleep. Many men who arrived back in England were in the same state.

But, as Clive says, in those days there were no therapists, no counsellors to take you to a quiet place and calm the memories of what you had seen. There was a war on, and the feeling in the country was that everyone had to 'do their bit'.

For a while, Clive and his comrades were rested well away from the action, in Scotland, and this gave him the chance to go flying for the first time. There is a cliché in the army that you should never volunteer for anything; Clive has always felt the opposite. He wanted the adventure. That attitude would land him some plum jobs, but also put him in a lot of danger.

After a short rest he became part of the 71st Field Company, Royal Engineers, and in doing so had to start the process of making friends all over again. For a while his duties were fairly straightforward, but soon the war intervened again and he was to face more death and destruction as Hitler sent the Luftwaffe to attack Britain.

Eventually we arrived at a small station outside Edinburgh. They had trucks ready for us, and we were taken to North Berwick, not far from the Musselburgh race course. We were billeted in empty houses – there was a whole row of them unused for some reason.

We were sent to the public baths to get clean at last; we hadn't washed all the way through France, into Dunkirk and on the boat.

We had a palliasse each to sleep on, and they kitted us out with new uniforms, just simple battle dress. Luckily I had my own boots and socks still.

We couldn't rest for too long though. They put us to work at a local aerodrome, working as a flare path party. They'd give each of us a lit paraffin lamp, and we'd set up the flare path for aircraft coming back after dark. They treated us like kings there, because we'd come from Dunkirk. I noticed that the Air Force people went to bed with a sheet and a blanket on their beds, not like we were used to, but they made sure we had them too. And when everyone was queuing for food, we went right to the front, even though some of them moaned a bit.

The young station commander, he can only have been twenty-five, was really nice to us, and wanted to be friendly. He said, 'If any of you boys would like a trip in a plane, put your name down in the company office and I'll make sure something is done.'

Now most of the other blokes in my outfit were quite a bit older than me, in fact when they weren't calling me Stinker I was known as Nipper. And they weren't so bothered about going in a plane, so in the end it was just me and one of my mates who wrote our names on the sheet. We were called one lunchtime, and they told us to be in the company office the next morning. We were going to go in an old bomber which had been converted into a weather aircraft, to test the conditions over the North Sea.

I'd never been in an aeroplane before. We sat by some windows in the fuselage, the weather was lovely and we really enjoyed ourselves. When we landed, we said thank you, and the commander said if we wanted to go again we should just say so. The other bloke wasn't bothered, but I said, 'Yes please sir!' straight away.

I suppose about three days later I was summoned to his office. He told me that he was going to take his two-seater fighter for a test flight the next day, after it had been serviced. Would I like to come? Of course I said yes.

So there I was, the next morning. He gave me a leather flying helmet and a leather jacket. We started off by climbing higher and higher, which gave me white knuckles because it was much faster than the old bomber we'd been in before. Then all of a sudden he banked right over while I was sat there enjoying the view, and he banked again, then he bloody looped and threw us all over the sky. I was bloody terrified!

After he'd done all that, he dropped down towards the aerodrome. It had telephone poles leading away from the buildings towards the main gate, and he flew so low that we went underneath them! We were so close. These young fighter pilots were fearless, guts of iron. I'm not easily frightened, but I was that day! When we finally stopped, he slid the canopy off and called my name. He said, 'Righto, out you get, Clive!' I managed to get my leg out onto the wing, then the next one, then I collapsed! My legs gave way and I fell right over onto the grass! He was laughing his bloody head off. He said, 'If you want another go, just let me know.'

'Not bloody likely, sir!' I said, even though he was an officer. Of course everyone in the aerodrome laughed about that for ages.

Later we got moved to Northern Ireland, to place called Aldergrove, because they wanted engineers. We were on flare path duty again, but as Dunkirk veterans they treated us well. Then one day we were told to jump in a truck because we were going to Belfast to pick up some ammunition. We got to Belfast and loaded up a couple of trucks. We were sitting in the back on the way home, when suddenly someone fired at us! We heard it coming in, although we couldn't see where it was coming from. Even though we had our rifles, we couldn't shoot back. The Air Force boys put their foot down, and we got back in one piece. Apparently it was the IRA having a go at us. They weren't very good shots! We laughed it off.

After some time in Ireland we went back to our base in Scotland, but soon afterwards everything changed. We were off to London. The Blitz had started.

Chapter Six

THE BLITZ

The Blitz, in the autumn and winter of 1940 to 1941, was Hitler's way of bringing the war to the people of Britain. It was born of frustration, after his bombers and fighters had failed to beat the RAF in the Battle of Britain.

Intent on invading, Hitler knew he would have to get the RAF out of the skies so that his invasion barges, already stockpiled on the northern coasts of France, could sail across the Channel safe from aerial attack.

During the long, hot summer, bombers flew countless raids over the English Channel, heading towards the RAF bases scattered along the south coast of England. The intention was either to destroy the British fighters on the ground, or tempt them up into the sky where they could be shot down.

The Luftwaffe famously failed to achieve its aims, although most historians agree it was a close-run thing. A series of ferocious battles in early September showed the Germans that the RAF was still a force to be reckoned with. With autumn fast approaching, Hitler was forced to accept that the invasion would have to be postponed. From daytime attacks on RAF bases, the target was changed. In what many saw as a tactical mistake, the Luftwaffe started making night attacks on major cities instead: London in particular. From 7 September the city was attacked for fifty-seven nights in a row.

The aim was to crush the will of the people, to make them push their politicians to surrender rather than face more bombs. Egged on by the head of the Luftwaffe, Hermann Goering, Hitler believed the British could be forced to capitulate.

But he had reckoned without the famous 'Blitz Spirit' – the indomitable ability of the British simply to suffer and keep a stiff upper lip. As the bombs rained down, Londoners made either for their hastily-built Anderson shelters in the garden, the communal shelters in parks and public places, or, famously, to the tube stations spread across the city.

Air raid wardens would tell you to 'put that light out!' West End shows continued, shops re-opened despite having no windows left, and women operated anti-aircraft guns. Even the Royal Family was affected, as Buckingham Palace was bombed. Far from crushing the will of the people, the Blitz united them in the belief that 'Britain can take it'.

But there was a terrible price to pay. The East End in particular saw many casualties as the Germans attacked the nearby docks. Hospitals, schools, pubs and churches across the city were hit, killing hundreds and thousands of men, women and children. Many of the city's most important buildings were destroyed, in scenes reminiscent of the Great Fire of London.

When the bombers had left, and dawn broke each morning, the heartbreaking and backbreaking job of looking for survivors in the rubble began in earnest. Volunteers made human chains to pass the broken remains of buildings away from the worst areas. Anyone who could wield a crowbar or pickaxe got to work to help those who were trapped. Often it was too late.

And of course there were the most dangerous problems; the bombs which had fallen but not exploded. They would bury themselves several feet into the ground, some of them capable of blowing up a whole street.

To help to move the biggest piles of rubble, and to dig out the most dangerous of the bombs, the army called in the Engineers. Clive was about to experience some of the worst – and best – times of his war.

We were stationed near Catford; I think it was in Herne Hill. We were there for general purposes, mainly to repair bomb damage. There were no beds for us, so we slept on the floor in an old school.

The biggest job we had was just outside Lewisham Hospital. They had dropped a bomb right in the middle of the road, and it had broken through the sewer. Now those pipes were big enough to stand up in, so you can imagine what a job that was. It was made of brick, and the blast had blown everything upstream and downstream. We had to dig it all out into containers, which were taken away in trucks. It was a stinking job, shovelling God knows what.

But the funny thing was, the whistle would blow, and you'd hear the call 'NAAFI up!' You'd climb out of the hole, and go and get your tea and a rock cake. No washing your hands or anything like that, none of today's Health and Safety. It was disgusting, with all the waste coming out of the hospital.

We were there for a couple of weeks because it was such a big job.

Then we were sent all over London to dig for unexploded bombs. We were shown where they were, then we had to dig down for them. We didn't defuse them, we just had to dig down and find them. You had to dig around them, in the soggy wet mud that made up the London soil. We were a right state by the end of each job, because you'd find the tail fin then have to go right down past it so people could get at it. We were young, and didn't have the time or the brains to think how dangerous it was. We'd signed up to do a job, and that's what we had to do. A couple of the boys lost it, and we never saw them again. Some others shot themselves in the foot, just to get out of it. But if I think about it honestly, in some strange way I actually enjoyed it. I know I'd signed on for King and Country, but believe me you soon forget that and it's all about self-preservation. You're not thinking about King and Country, you're thinking about Clive Kemp! And anyway you couldn't say no.

One time we thought we were about three-quarters of the way down to a bomb, digging hard in the mud. Now at that time you were lucky if you got one bath a week. Where we were staying, there was one basin between twelve of you, and all the water was cold. Then all of a sudden they said, 'Right you lot, into the truck, we're taking you to the local baths.' So off we went in the truck, they gave us a towel and some soap, and we had a good old clean even though we thought we'd have to go back to the dirty great hole we were digging. But while we were there, someone came in and told us that the bomb we had been digging out had just exploded, while we were bathing! I'm sure we would all have been killed if we had been there.

Me (left) hard at work during the Blitz

Another time, shortly before we left London, we started digging for another one. You could see the hole where it had gone in, and we had followed it about eight or ten feet down. Then there was the cry, 'NAAFI!' so we got out for a cup of tea and a wad, as we used to call it. We were standing there outside the cordon eating and drinking when *Whump!* Up it went. I'd escaped again. We treated it lightly, 'Christ! Another lucky one!' and thought nothing of it. How bloody stupid. When you are young, the adrenaline is pumping all the time, you just get on with it.

I can remember watching the bombers flying up the Thames; they used to use it to get their bearings. One time they bombed a great big timber yard which caught fire, and I've never seen anything like it. It was awful. We could see the dogfights going on as the RAF fighters attacked them. I just stood there, my head up and my mouth open, watching.

We were sent to a block of flats that had been bombed, near the Surrey Docks. They wanted us to bring out the bodies. That was really terrible. The state of the women and children. I cried. I still do. I carried this little kiddie ... I still can't bear to think about it.

To get over it, people played practical jokes. One time they propped a body up against a wall, and just as I went past it moved. What do you do? You laugh, you have to, at someone else's misfortune. The amount of death I saw was dreadful, but this was the first time I'd seen many civilians killed. From then on, I hated the Germans, they were bastards, and I just wanted to get in and get after them.

Soon they found out that I'd worked for a gas company. They asked me if I was any good at repairing broken gas pipes. Now I'd seen it done, but had never done it myself. I knew the theory from my City and Guilds exams. They gave me six blokes, a truck, and all the supplies I needed.

Now what you had to do was to dig down and find the broken ends of the pipe. Then you drilled a hole in the top of the intact bit of the pipe, and pushed in an old football bladder. You blew it up, and that would stop the gas. You would do the same on the other broken part, then cut off the damaged bit. All you had to do then was put a new piece of pipe between them, which was then sealed with a special collar and some lead. Pull out the bladders, plug the holes you drilled after getting the bladders out, and that was it. For all this danger we used to get a penny a day extra pay!

Now the people of London who we were helping were always very friendly towards us. We were working on this one gas main for several days, and I kept seeing these two nice birds going past. In those days you'd get one day off a week after working until the evening, so of course it was always, 'Hello love, what are you doing tonight?'

Eventually one of the girls said, 'Well I'm off tonight. We live over there. Meet us at seven o'clock!' They were sisters, one each for me and my mate. Goodness they treated us well. The grub we had, they must have been on the black market. They had corned beef, lots of tea, and we had a great time.

Then they took us out. Now, I'm not a drinker, I'd never drunk, but these girls took us out to a pub called the Barley Mow. We walked up there arm in arm, not a care in the world. My girl ordered brown ale, and

I couldn't be seen drinking lemonade could I? So I ended up drinking brown ale too. Kick out time came, and the girls said, 'Come on Clive, back with us, we'll put you up for the night.' They had a brother who was in the army, so they had a spare room. So I got dragged home! I remember my boots had really shiny toes because I used to polish them with a toothbrush handle and some spit. It really was spit and polish in those days. Anyway, by the time they'd dragged me back to their house my lovely toecaps were all shredded!

They must have put us to bed; I think I slept on the floor and my mate was on the bed.

Then in the morning, the girls had got up early and gone to work. Their mum came in, bright and breezy, saying, 'Right then boys, who's for some breakfast?' But the way my bloody head was, I said I didn't think I could eat any. She wasn't having it though, and she said, 'You're going to have some breakfast!' She was lovely, friendly, a well-made woman.

For some reason my mate didn't want to go back there, but I went back whenever I was off, because I found that more than just breakfast was on the menu, if you know what I mean!

One night I was there and a raid came over. Me and my girl went outside because we thought it might be safer if an incendiary came down. We were there snogging in the doorway when her old man came out yelling, 'What's the bloody door rattling for?' He was a proper rough one. He worked cleaning buses all night, and would come home early in the morning swearing his head off.

The girls were working on munitions somewhere, and I went to see them whenever I could. One time I arrived and my girl wasn't back. Her mum offered me breakfast again, then asked if I fancied a lie-down after all my hard work. Well, we forgot about the breakfast, and had a good lie-down together!

Then, believe it or not, I arrived another time and nobody was in. But the auntie who lived next door heard me knocking and invited me in. And she looked after me very well too!

I was quite busy in London, all told ...

Members of the London Fire Brigade train their hoses on burning buildings during the Blitz © IWM HU 1129

In the aftermath of a bombing raid, a bus lies in a crater in Balham, south London. 'I saw things like this all the time during the Blitz.' © IWM HU 36188

Chapter Seven

TRAINING

Clive had started the war as a nineteen-year-old lad from a small island. He was now a veteran of two terrible battles, and had seen more death and destruction than most. As things stabilised on the Home Front with the end of the Blitz, the country's leaders had to start to focus on how they could win the war.

While the threat of invasion had now passed, the war was still going very badly. Britain was fighting virtually alone, with its supply lines threatened by the submarines which stalked the ships coming across the Atlantic.

Only when Hitler turned his attention to Russia, making his fatal attack in June 1941, and America entered the war in December the same year after the bombing of Pearl Harbour, could the country have the breathing space and resources it needed.

It meant that the 71st Field Company could retrain as a specialist unit. Its specialism was to be bridging, and this would put it at the spearhead of the future invasion and drive across France.

Any advance by an army can only go ahead if the road is clear. If that road is interrupted by a river or other obstacle whose bridges have been destroyed, the advance grinds to a halt. If the tanks and troops are to be able to get across, new bridges have to be built, and fast. Consequently, engineering outfits follow the advance very closely, ready to build crossings immediately, often under heavy fire. After all, the enemy will know exactly where any bridges will be built, and will be able to concentrate their artillery and machine guns there.

Speed was of the essence, and so the 71st Field Company would have to practise and practise again to become as efficient as possible. For Clive that meant hours, days, and weeks of carrying and fixing parts of what became known as Bailey bridges.

They were named after their inventor Donald Bailey, and had several advantages for the army. They were relatively light, so they could be transported easily. They were made in sections, so they could be made to any length. And perhaps most importantly, they could be put together by manpower alone; they didn't need cranes or specialist tools.

Essentially, they were a series of linked, floating pontoons with raised latticed supports on the sides. Sections of men were able to carry each part and put them together, rather like a giant Meccano set. Extra pieces could be floated out on to the river, pulled into place using a motorboat, then simply bolted together. It was hard work for the men involved, but a well-drilled team could build a Bailey bridge much faster than they could build a traditional one.

These skills were what Clive had to learn in the next three years of his war; he spent his time training while the war went on.

In Russia, Hitler stormed towards Moscow, getting as far as the capital's outlying underground stations, only to suffer the fate of Napoleon before him. Like the French Emperor, his advance ground to a halt, and was pushed back by the sheer mass of men the Russians threw at it. The long retreat led to some of the most barbaric fighting of the war.

In the desert, Rommel seemed unbeatable in pushing the British Eighth Army back, until the battle of El Alamein began to turn the tide, ending in defeat for the Axis.

In the Far East, Japanese forces were becoming known for their savage treatment of Allied prisoners and suicidal courage in attack and defence.

While this was happening, the planners of D-Day were hard at work. The Allies knew that the only way to win the war was to throw the Germans out of Europe. They would have to invade France. Hundreds of thousands of men, with tons and tons of equipment and machinery, would have to cross the Channel. Clive would be one of them, a tiny cog in the vast invasion machine.

When the Blitz finally came to an end, they decided to move us up country. We ended up based in the Ipswich area for training, and we spent the next couple of years learning all sorts of skills.

One of the things they did was to send us to a place in the West Country called Porlock. They didn't say much about it, but I think it was a place for chemical weapons training. On our uniform was a white, green and yellow striped square, which denoted chemical warfare. There were rockets there, which reminded me of the German moaning minnies. We ended up taking them down to Dartmoor for test firing. They weren't armed of course.

I had a funny experience there. All through the war I was the youngest in our outfit, so I used to get 'volunteered' to do things by the older blokes. And when they were firing off these great big rockets I had to go and stand in the area where they thought they would land, to see if they had been on target.

Anyway, this one time, me and a couple of mates were waiting for ages and the fog came down, really thick, and we couldn't move because we didn't know the way back. No food, nothing. No sleeping bags. So we huddled up together for warmth, and had to wait to be rescued! They sent some blokes out to get us in the end.

I don't think they continued with the rockets, because they weren't powerful enough or something. And I'm glad, because it would have meant chemical warfare, which is bloody dangerous!

Then I was back to Ipswich, to learn more about making bridges.

We were kicked out of bed at all times of the night, thrown in the back of lorries no matter what the weather, and driven to God knows where to build a bridge. I think I must have built bridges across every river in England, Scotland and Wales! We were training so hard, we were all so fit, and we could see the other people around us were getting fit and ready too. We could build a bridge blindfold. We'd stay away from base for a week or so, then go back again. Then they'd call us out in the middle of the night to go and build an emergency crossing, and off we'd have to go, whatever the weather. I remember one officer used to be called 'Skidchain Charlie', because as soon as it got a bit muddy he'd make us fit chains onto the wheels of our vehicles. His actual name was Lieutenant Colonel Lloyd.

A Bailey bridge is just like a great big Meccano set, and was really hard work to put together. We used to curse old Skidchains because he worked us so hard, but we knew we were getting better at it.

When you start, you have to clear a space around the river bank first. Then you get the first bit of the bridge on rollers, and roll it into the water, like launching a ship. Then each of the new bits would be floated out on pontoons and joined on the end. Of course each of the parts was very, very heavy. Six of us on each side would grab the pieces to carry it. I'd have sores on the inside of my elbows from the work. I remembered my father's warnings that I would rue the day I joined up! Of course, being a short-arse it was even harder for me. So later on in the war, when we were in France and they said they wanted someone to be a motorboat driver I said yes please! But in the meantime we made sure that everyone could do everybody else's job. We were all pretty expert really. In fact, we were so good that we got chosen to build the first bridge in France, at Pegasus.

We also had to learn how to get rid of mines. We were never meant to lay them, but had to learn how to get rid of them in case there weren't enough assault pioneers around where we had to make our bridge. You'd have a squad of three. The first one of you had the detector, which you'd wave over the ground. It would whistle if there was a mine underneath. If there was, you'd point it out to the next bloke, who would mark it for you. Then the bloke behind him would lift it out of the ground. It was bloody hard though, and you'd have to change places every twenty minutes. The sweeper would go back to be the lifter, and so on, and you'd keep going.

We did lots of PT – abseiling, cliff climbing. I remember they used to teach us unarmed combat, these great big blokes, and we had to disarm them and things like that. Talk about Kung Fu, they'd just chuck me up in the air because I'm so small. Then they'd march us into a gym, divide us into two rows, left and right, then we would have to do three rounds in the boxing ring with the bloke opposite you. Most of them were so much taller than me they only had to hold their hands out and I couldn't get near them! In a funny way I enjoyed it all, even though they used to knock six kinds of shit out of you. It was all part of the training, even though I never ended up using it, I never got close enough.

We also had to learn how to cross rivers on ropes. One day we were taken to a river somewhere between London and Reading; it might even have been the Thames. The river was about twenty five feet wide, and running pretty fast. Someone had built some little platforms next to the river bank on either side. Across the river they had stretched two ropes, one for us to stand on, and one about seven feet above that for us to hold on to with our arms up. They were thick and strong ropes, pulled really tight. The rope you stood on was about ten feet above the water. The idea was that you would slide along with your hands on the top rope, shuffling your feet along sideways until you got to the other side. We were all loaded down with small pack, steel helmet, and a rifle slung across our back.

We gathered on one side of the bank. There were two of us who were much younger than the rest of them, and we always wanted to be first, being keen and brainless. He was from Devon, and shaped like a dumpling, everyone used to laugh at his accent. Anyway, we tossed a coin to see which one of us would go first, to get it over with, and he won.

He started off, and I think he must have got about six or eight feet along, and then he lost his balance. When that happens on that sort of river crossing, your feet go from under you, and you end up lying stretched on your back with your feet out in front, trying to hold on. I was just a short way behind him, and of course because he was pushing the ropes sideways I was going over backwards too. I was pushing the other way, trying to get us back upright, but his weight was too much for me. I was saying 'stand up, stand up,' but he said 'I can't', and the next thing I knew, he let go and fell in. As soon as he did that, the ropes wobbled really badly, and I started to panic. The officers on the bank were shouting at me, and I had to try to get back upright. Eventually I managed it, but I still had to get to the other side of the river. My whole body was tired, especially my hands, and I could hardly move, but finally I got across. I fell to my knees and cheered, because I had been so scared. Meanwhile, two of the officers had dived in to try to save the lad who had fallen in. They searched and searched but they never found him. It was such a shame, he had only just come back from leave in Devon, where he had got married. It didn't stop the exercise though; everyone else had to go across the rope bridge, even though he'd been lost. I think they might have tightened the ropes first, but they all had to do it.

To try and keep our morale up we used to make our own fun; there we were, a bunch of blokes living and working together very closely. Often if someone left their boots or steel helmet out at night, someone else in the tent would take a pee in them. Then the next morning, or even in the middle of the night, we'd be called to action. They'd ram their feet into their boots, or put their helmet on in a hurry, and splat! I always kept mine safe, didn't leave anything out that could be peed in.

Another thing you'd do, if you were in tents and it was raining, was to run your finger down the inside of the tent above the bloke in the next bed. The water would get through and drip on his face! Or we'd creep out in the middle of the night and let down the ropes on the next tent so it collapsed on them.

Most of us would have one mate in particular, one bloke who you would team up with if you were going out, share food with if you were short, or help out if they had a hard job to do. My best mate was Ernie Rice. He was a bit of a rough diamond.

Once I had a bit of leave coming up and I didn't know where to spend it, or what to do with myself. I told him I might go to London and stay at the Union Jack Club or something. But he said, 'Why don't you come up to Manchester with me? I've got seven days off too.' So that was the plan. We got on the train, and headed up to Manchester. We walked about half a mile from the station with our big heavy kitbags, and ended up at his house. He opened the door, and the first thing he's greeted with is, 'Oh, you're effing back!'

And he said, 'Yes I am! Why?!'

'Well,' she says, 'I don't want you here, you're an effing pain in the arse!'

And she was coming out with all these terrible things, and they had a right bloody set-to! There's me standing behind him not knowing what to say. After about ten minutes of them having a go at each other, he said, 'Right, I'm off to my sisters down the road. I'm not having this. But she won't have room for this mate of mine that I've brought with me. He'll have to sleep here.'

There's me thinking, 'Oh my God, what have I let myself in for?' So I got my stuff and said to her, 'I'll just sleep on the sofa if that's all right with you?'

'Sleep where you bloody like!' she replied.

I don't think I even undressed, I just took off my cap and boots and tried to get some sleep. When he came round in the morning, he said, 'Hello, Clive, did you have a good night?'

And she went off again then, 'He just bloody slept down here all night, he didn't even want to come upstairs!' I didn't even know what was upstairs, maybe there was a spare room or something. I told him it was all a bit awkward for me, and maybe I'd just head down to my sister's place in Guildford instead. 'Oh do what you bloody like.' he said.

So that was me off like a shot, straight to the station and away.

He was a good bloke though, and a good friend to have in the army. He'd do anything for anyone, and he was a very hard worker. If there was any trouble he was there, even though he was only a short little bloke. He was quite stocky though, and could handle himself if the Canadians started any fights. I'd always want to get out and get away, but he'd always say, 'No, we can hold our own.' I told him he could hold his own if he wanted, I was off!

Another bloke I got friendly with later was Stan Sharman. He's the only other one of us still alive as I write this. He's ninety-three. He was a really nice man, someone you just had to like. But that also meant he was easy to take the mickey out of. I remember one night in Scotland we were billeted in these houses, somewhere in North Berwick I think. We'd always look for a room big enough to get us and our palliasses into. This one night I woke up thinking I could hear water. I looked up and there he was, stark naked, just starting to have a pee up against the door! I shouted, 'Stan! What the bloody hell are you doing?'

'Oh Christ!' he said.

He'd been asleep, and hadn't woken up when he went for his pee; my shout had woken him up! I knew what was happening because a brother of mine used to do the same. He asked me not to tell anyone. And he was such a nice bloke, I didn't want to upset him. He had very different ideas about things to me. He always wanted to listen to highbrow music, which I thought was a load of rubbish. I used to tease him about it. I probably took the mickey out of him more than I did out of anybody else. If I needed a pee in the middle of the night, sometimes I'd reach for his steel helmet, or his wellington boots. Other people had done the same to me, after all! It would make him late on parade because he had to sort all his stuff out. I remember tying the laces at the top of his kitbag with hundreds of knots, so it took him ages to get into it. Again, late on parade!

It wasn't a very nice thing to do, I suppose, but we were in a different environment then, and it's what you did. There was nothing going on, nothing to do except train, train, train, and we had to find ways to let off steam. It was all just schoolboy pranks really. He would always laugh about it afterwards, and never tried to get you back for it. He was like me, really, in that he never wanted to get into fights or anything like that.

Sometimes, to break the boredom, a company officer would organise a village hall or church hall or something, and would tell us he wanted to hold a concert. 'I'd like you chaps to do your bit,' he'd say, hoping we'd all put our names down to do an act. Sometimes the villagers would join in, playing a bit of piano, or singing or dancing. My mate Stan's speciality was a song called 'Brown Boots', and he sang it all the bloody time. Every time he came on stage to start singing at one of these concerts, the whole company would join in and start singing with him. He'd get annoyed, and stop, and tell us all to shut up because it was a solo. But of course we never did, and we always sang and heckled him all the way. He'd laugh about it afterwards.

Quite a few of the blokes had some kind of act they could do; some would play the spoons or the harmonica, have a song or do a tap dance. Often they'd sing rude army songs which the officers didn't like because of the civilians there. The officers would say, 'Not too much of that, boys!' but for a lot of the blokes it was all they knew.

Any time we had a night off, me and the boys would go out boozing. Having said that, I never really drank, so I'd always buy my round but just drink lemonade. We'd go looking for birds too, just for some company. Of course if any of them came on too strong I'd always say no! We always respected them, and really just wanted some friendship to take our minds off things.

Because I'd been at Dunkirk I was seen as a bit of a veteran by this lot. I'd seen death, faced bombs and bullets, and gone off on the boat. They sometimes asked me what it was like, how I'd coped, and whether I could give them any advice about how to face it all. I told them about the lines of refugees, the scream of the bombs, and how to avoid getting hit by lying flat. I told them that if they were in a truck and they heard a Jerry plane, to get out quick, and get into a ditch. I could already recognise the difference in sounds between German and British planes.

For a while we were stationed in a place called Margam Castle, in Wales. It was beautiful, and looked a bit like Jersey's Victoria College. It had this orangery, like a big greenhouse, where we were all bunked down. Now the entrance to the castle was about a quarter of a mile down a long drive. Just outside the castle was a little hut where you would be based if you were on guard. Six or eight of us were on duty at any time, for about two hours each. Alongside this driveway to the castle were little graveyards, with the graves of people who had lived and died there.

One night when I was on guard, at about two in the morning I walked down the drive to relieve the bloke who was on duty at the end. And it was really foggy, you couldn't see very well, and I started to feel really apprehensive. I got to the end and whistled for the other bloke. He answered me, and did the usual, 'Halt, who goes there?' I answered him and off he went into the fog. So I was standing there leaning against the gatepost, feeling a bit scared and thinking bad thoughts. Around that time we'd had lectures that there were German parachutists dropping all over the country for reconnaissance, dressed as nuns and whatnot. And I had all that in my head while I was standing there on my own in the silence. Then, at about half past three or four o'clock, there was a rustle of leaves near me, and Christ! I jumped, and pulled the bloody trigger. Of course all my mates came running down to find out what was going on, and we realised it was one of the local dogs who had been snuffling about in a ditch! He had run off, but came back again when my mates arrived.

Funnily enough, while I was in Margam I had another coincidental meeting. A little train runs across the centre of the town, and I was there one day when the barrier went down so the train could cross. So I stopped and looked across the road; and there were two Jersey girls! Their mum was from Margam, and they'd all gone there when the war started. I shouted across to them. We got chatting, and they invited me back to their house that night, for Jersey bean crock! It made me very homesick, but I still borrowed a motorbike to go and visit them again.

I always tried to look immaculate. Here I am in my Blues (dress uniform).

Another time, at Newport in Wales, I was given fourteen days confined to barracks for being cheeky. I remember the headquarters building there had seventy-eight steps going up to it. And every night I used to have to scrub every bloody step, changing the water half way up. Once this officer stopped me and said, 'That looks like hard work, your arms must be worn out Kemp!'

'Yes sir, is there any chance of a cup of tea?' I replied.

I was always in trouble; late back to camp, being cheeky to officers, saying something under my breath: 'I heard that, Kemp!' and I'd get seven days.

Another thing that got me into trouble at Newport was my uniform. I was always well turned out, and a bit vain. I'd got this girl to adapt my kit for me a bit, and I had these five pleats ironed into the back of my battledress to make it look better. Anyway, this officer came along to inspect us, and he stopped behind me and said, 'You're out of order, Kemp!'

'Am I sir?'

'Yes, these pleats in your uniform!'

I told him I was only trying to be smart. 'Well you're too bloody smart!' he said, 'Iron them flat!'

Another time, this girl that I'd met helped me out. If you were a conscript, you weren't allowed to wear Blues, which was the name for a nice mess uniform. But if you'd volunteered, like me, you could. I saw this lovely set of Blues in a tailor's shop window, and told this girl how nice they were, and how I'd love to wear them. They were dark blue, with a red stripe up the legs. The only problem was that you needed all the right clothes coupons to get them. And this girl said she'd ask around her family and friends, to see if she could get enough coupons. I think I needed seven. It didn't take long for me to get them.

Now quite often we'd get an invitation to a dance in the area where we were billeted, and we could wear Blues if we were entitled to. So I turned up to this dance, and our sergeant major was there too, also in his Blues. As soon as he saw me, he started shouting, 'What are you doing wearing Blues, Kemp? You're not entitled to wear them!' and his voice was really loud. I told him I was allowed to wear them. 'No you're not!' he replied, 'It's only commissioned officers and regulars who can wear them!'

So I said, 'I happen to be a regular, sir!'

'Have you got proof of that?' he shouted.

'Yes I have sir,' I said, and I pulled out my pay book which I always kept in my breast pocket. 'There you are,' I said, 'I'm a regular, in for six and six!' I really enjoyed knocking him down like that. I have to say he didn't seem to bear me a grudge afterwards; he didn't do me any harm because of it.

I suppose even though I was often a bit cheeky like this, the officers were quite sympathetic to me because I was from Jersey. And once we got back to France, I was never really in trouble. Eventually I got married in those Blues, after a real coincidence which happened while we were training.

My mum in Jersey was allowed to contact me through the Red Cross. She used to send me letters and things, to tell me she was all right. And in one, she asked me if I knew where my cousin Doreen was. You see, she'd left Jersey before the Occupation, but her parents were still there. Now I used to get a little newsletter called the Channel Islands Review, that an aunt of mine used to send me. It was full of little bits of information about the islands, and she used to circle anything she thought might be interesting to me. So I put a little advert in, asking if anyone knew where a Miss Doreen Ahier was, and if so to please get in touch. Eventually Doreen herself did, and told me where she lived, in Paignton. We wrote a few times, and we got more informal every time. Eventually I went down to meet her, and she was lovely, very pretty. To cut a long story short, we finally got married in Guildford, close to where my sister lived. Some other people who had left Jersey came too. A Mr Burke, who used to run a newsagent in Halkett Place, invited us round to his new place in Guildford. As we were leaving, his lovely wife said, 'Here, you'd better take this with you!' and she gave us this great big wedding cake, all covered in icing. We'd never have been able to afford one ourselves.

After our wedding, we went to London to meet another Jersey lady called Mrs Masterman, and we stayed with her. Us newlyweds were keen to get upstairs to bed of course, but all of a sudden a bloody air raid starts. Now I was used to that by this time, and I was just going to take it in my stride. What I didn't know was that there was an ack-ack gun right outside the window, and that went off with a great CRASH! And I was out of that bloody bed and under it in an instant! And my wife was still in bed laughing at me! I said it was because of my natural soldier's instinct ...

We did have some serious work to do though. We were in Hastings when some Jerry planes came skimming over the Channel at wave height, and shot up some of the houses on the front, dropping a couple of bombs as they went. They called us down to the site to help. It was wicked to see the damage they'd done; there was water everywhere, and I had to deal with gas which was escaping. We must have been based quite close to them, because we got there before the emergency services. I told one bloke to switch off the gas and electricity, just in case. There was a family of five dead inside: the parents and three kiddies under the age of ten, who we had to carry out of the house. That was horrible, very harrowing, and I was crying as I worked.

While we were training, the Americans started to arrive, to build runways for their Flying Fortresses. I don't know how or why, but they arranged for twelve of us to go and live and work with them for a fortnight.

Now in the British Army there was a shortage of everything, we were living like hermits. But when we got to the Yanks' camp, you'll never believe the way they ate! The first evening we got there, fairly late, they got us a hot drink and turkey sandwiches. Turkey! In the middle of the war! The next morning there was a table, maybe twenty feet long, with all the fruit juices you could name on it. The Yanks didn't drink it, they used it as mouthwash! The first main meal was roast potatoes, vegetables, and half a bloody chicken each! And they said, 'If you want any more, just come and ask!' Now they drank coffee all the time, but we drank tea, so I asked one if they had any. 'Oh yeah, buddy,' he said, 'come with me.' And he gave me a sandbag full of tea! I tipped a load of it into a bucket to make us a big brew. And he said he had loads more, so when I left I could help myself! And he gave us tins of peaches, all sorts of things. You just couldn't imagine the difference in how they lived.

Another example is drainage. Now, if we were based somewhere and we had to make some drains, it would be out with the picks and shovels. They had a big machine going round driven by a laughing black guy, doing it all for them. They were so undisciplined, in fact I'd go as far as to say they were yellow.

They built the hangers first, to keep all their stuff in. There must have been three hundred camp beds along the sides for them to sleep in. They mixed me and my mates up among them so we could get to know each other.

Anyway, the first night we were there the sirens went, for a raid. And me and my mates nearly got killed in the bloody rush! We were lying there, and they were jumping all over the place, tipping over their beds, you'd never seen anything like it. Of course, after the Blitz, we were used to it.

But it was the same later in the war, on the Rhine. As soon as the guns started, the Yanks were the first to leg it. We always stayed until it got hot. And around Caen, after D-Day, their bombers always used to drop their loads and turn around when the ack-ack came up, but the RAF used to fly straight through it. We could never have won the war without the Yankee stuff, but we might have won it without the men!

They were generous though, because they could afford to be. They would give you the earth, because they had it to give.

Later in the war, we were training around Guildford, and we were around a lot of Canadians. They were different again, very big and very big-headed. They would always elbow you out of the way, especially in a bar. The number of fights I saw ... I didn't take part because I'm so small, I would always be out of the bloody window when things kicked off.

And with all the extra stuff the Americans and Canadians had, they always got the best birds. What they said about them being over-paid, over-sexed and over here was right! Their uniforms were much smarter than ours, and we didn't usually get a look in. But I wasn't always unlucky; I had a good story to tell. I was from Jersey, I couldn't go home, and they felt sorry for me!

But I suppose we were glad to see the Americans. We'd been thrown out of France, and we knew we'd have to go back there to win the war; that's what we were training for. And seeing all this stuff arriving, all these bombers and lorries and tanks, and all the blokes, that made us think that something was really happening. We never said to each other, 'Well, we'll win the war now,' because we had never doubted that anyway.

All the time we were training, we never knew anything about what was planned by the top brass. We didn't know we were off to D-Day until we were put into a barbed wire camp.

Just before that our major, who felt sorry for me because I was from Jersey, tried to help me out. He sent me and four of my mates off with a lorry full of ammunition and explosives. He'd picked out a place in the countryside in Hampshire, and he told us to go to a particular map reference, dig a hole, and bury it safely. We had to bivvy there for a few days. The major said we would probably miss D-Day, because they'd be going while we were away. I was from Jersey, the other four blokes were all married men too, and I think he was trying to save us.

Anyway, we got there and dug a great big hole to bury all this stuff. We packed it all in nicely, covered it over and put a tarpaulin over the top to camouflage it. We were told to wait there for a few days, until after D-Day, and then we'd have to get going again.

But when the word came to move, D-Day still hadn't happened. And we had a big problem. We went to get the ammunition out, only to find the hole had filled with water, and everything was bloody soaked! And in the end of course we went in on D-Day even though we were registered to go two days later, on D+2. We went back to our sealed camp, and everyone knew the invasion was coming, although no one told us where we were going or what we'd have to do until we got on the boat.

Chapter Eight

D-DAY

The attack on the Normandy beaches on 6 June 1944 is rightly recognised as one of the pivotal moments in modern history. For months the Allies had been stockpiling men and equipment on the south coast of England. Vast camps had been created, where men could live cut-off from the outside world, in case they gave away secrets. Most of them, including Clive, knew very little anyway. For many of them, their destination was uncertain until they were actually on board ship.

The French coast of Normandy had been chosen for the invasion for several reasons. Firstly, it wasn't the obvious place – its beaches are much further away from England than those in the Pas de Calais, where you can actually see across from one country to the other.

But the best reason was that it had ideal landing beaches. They were relatively flat for the most part, and attackers would be able to get inland quickly once they had penetrated the beach defences, especially in the eastern area. The beaches were also predominantly sandy, which meant that they were easier to move on than shingle or rocky beaches.

The beaches were divided into five sections. The Americans, on the western flank, would attack the edge of the Cherbourg peninsula at Utah Beach, and immediately below that at Omaha. Mixed forces of Canadians and British troops could take on the eastern side of the invasion, on beaches named Gold, Juno and Sword.

But the planners had to look inland too. They knew that once the invading forces got ashore, they would only be able to press ahead if the roads were clear; and that of course meant that bridges had to be secured. One of the most famous actions of D-Day was conceived because of this.

Pegasus Bridge crosses the Caen canal, part-way between Caen and Sword Beach. The canal, parallel to the River Orne, runs roughly north to south. If you cross Pegasus going east, you come to the Orne River Bridge. About five miles from the invasion beaches, these two bridges were the Allies' first targets on D-Day.

They were important for two very good reasons. Firstly, if all went to plan, the invaders would make their way inland from the beaches. The canal and river were at their eastern edge. In order to attack the German forces to the east, the Allied forces would have to cross them with their tanks, guns and men. On the other hand, if the invasion didn't go so well, the Germans would be sure to counter-attack. Several key enemy divisions were based to the south and east of the River Orne, and would have to cross it to get close to the beachheads. Either way, for attack or defence, the invaders needed to control the bridges.

In his book *Pegasus Bridge*, Stephen E. Ambrose quotes Panzer General Hans von Luck as saying that if the Orne bridges had been available to him, his regiment of the 21st Panzer Division would have been able to attack the beaches on the afternoon of D-Day.

But in an astonishing *coup de main*, parachutists and glider troops landed right next to the bridges shortly after midnight on 6 June. After a short fight, the Germans guarding them were routed, and Major John Howard was able to send the famous signal 'Ham and Jam', meaning they had taken them both. One of the parachutists that night, later badly wounded in the fight for Normandy, was a PT instructor from the Midlands called Sid Peck. Nearly sixty years later, living in Jersey, he would become one of Clive's best friends in the Normandy Veterans Association. In the same aircraft as Sid was a lieutenant named Richard Todd, who would in later years become a famous actor.

The Germans tried to counter-attack, but the Paras fought them off with help from the guns of battleships anchored offshore. Finally, when their ammunition was running dangerously low, they heard the sound of bagpipes. The Commandos had arrived from the beaches, linking the beachhead with the bridges, and saving them for the Allies.

Clive, meanwhile, had his own adventures. He'd jumped into the water at the very eastern end of the invading forces, at Ouistreham. That little town was the focus of heavy fighting, especially around the casino. But his orders, with 71st Field Company, were to get inland as fast as possible, without stopping to fight, and get to Pegasus Bridge. The idea was that if it had been destroyed, his Company would build a replacement as quickly as possible.

Clive and his comrades were the front-runners of the Engineers, and were not carrying any heavy equipment. Their job was to get to the bridge fast, to begin surveying operations, before all the bridging material caught up with them later. They raced south in their lorries, supported by a Bren gun carrier, going past the bridge and the nearby chateau to find the spot where they had to start work. They were exposed to enemy fire all the time, and Clive lost one of his best friends to a vigilant sniper. His unit made one of the deepest penetrations into France that day, as fighting held up the advance.

He arrived at the bridge before the Commandos, and remembers them turning up to the sound of pipes and cheering from the Paras. Some of the Paras who were there remember with amazement that a couple of lorries and a Bren gun carrier could have got there so quickly.

In memoirs published after the war, Richard Todd remembered the main Royal Engineers force arriving:

Sometime during the middle of the afternoon, the CO sent me to check on 'B' Company's position in and north of Le Port. Having done this, I walked up the road for a few hundred yards towards the coast to see if anything was heading in our direction. To my amazement, a convoy of three-ton lorries came trundling into view. The leading truck stopped, and a florid-faced, ginger-moustached RE major jumped out. He was in charge of a Royal Engineers bridging party and had simply collected his vehicles together off the beach and driven a couple of miles down the main road towards Caen, totally unaware that only the Commando brigade had gone before him. He asked me if the Orne bridges were intact and if the road to Caen was clear. I advised him to hang on and to have his men take up defensive positions. If a bunch of soft-skinned vehicles could have reached this far intact, where the hell were the expected forward invasion troops?

Although Pegasus and the Orne River bridges had been saved, Clive's orders were to get building a new crossing. Pegasus Bridge is narrow, and big military vehicles would only be able to cross in one direction. By building a new bridge a few hundred yards to the south, the Allies would be able to use one to take men and materiel east to continue the advance, while casualties could come back westwards to be evacuated from the beaches.

Clive stayed there until 11 July, building and then maintaining the bridge while waiting for the Allies to break out of the bridgehead. They were held up by German Panzer forces gathered in and around Caen, a city which had been a first-day objective.

In his off-duty moments, Clive, together with many other soldiers, spent time at the Café Gondrée. There in the café began a friendship which continues today. The rest of the time he spent in his billet next to the chateau, an imposing building which still has the row of trees where he dug his shelter in the garden. At the time, he didn't know that he had been part of one of the most important moments in history.

The original Pegasus Bridge was taken down in 1994. It was saved for posterity, and is now a central part of the museum which was built next to its modern replacement. Clive was asked to carry out the official opening.

All around us were miles and miles of lorries, miles and miles of tents, thousands and thousands of men milling around. We all knew something big was happening, but as usual none of us were told what.

On the journey down to Newhaven from the camp, I remember feeling very apprehensive because we didn't know where we were going or what we were getting into. I felt I had a slight advantage over the other blokes because I'd been to Dunkirk, but that didn't help very much.

Once we got to Newhaven, I was put on a landing ship tank, known as an LST. It was pretty horrible, because most of the lads in my unit had never been on a big ship; again, because of my past experiences I had quite an advantage. But soon the smell of the ship was terrible, there was vomit everywhere. The crew were giving out tins of Maconochie's soup, which I quite liked. And of course, being a cheeky bugger, I was taking the piss out of my mates, offering them open cans of this stuff, just to make them feel even more sick! To make matters worse we were delayed, because D-Day was postponed by a

Aged 23, just prior to D-Day

day. Of course we were kept on the boat, and we couldn't see out, and all the blokes were ill before we'd even left harbour.

Eventually, when we all settled, our major explained to us where we were going. He said that our mission would be to get to Bénouville, to Pegasus Bridge, and build another one across the canal if Pegasus had been knocked out. It was the bridge the Paras had been told to capture and hold overnight until they were relieved. If it had been captured and held, then we'd have to build another one upstream, so they could both work for us. We were told to just get there as fast as we could, then wait for the bridging stuff to arrive to get on with the job.

I found myself somewhere cosy to stay; I always did that whenever I could, to make sure I was comfortable. I crawled under a truck, which I thought would be quite a safe place if we were attacked.

When we finally got close to Sword Beach, we still couldn't really see what was happening unless one of us got onto another's shoulders. There was all sorts of stuff flying around. I don't know if a shell ever landed near us, but the noise was incredible. There were shells coming over from the Germans, aimed at us, and shells from our ships firing over at them. We were caught in the middle, and the sound was deafening. It was like fireworks night a thousand times over. Anyone who says they weren't scared is a liar. We were all hyped up, and hyped and scared go together.

Eventually the ramp went down, and the officers were yelling at us to get out as quickly as we could. Our little truck went off first. I followed it, carrying my Bren gun straight into the sea, and sank right up to my waist! Our officer was shouting, 'Run, Kemp, run!' and I turned round and shouted, 'How am I supposed to f***ing run?!' Anyway, I managed to wade onto the beach. I saw there was some firing coming from a building ahead, and I could see the flash from the muzzle. So I lay down on the sand, and I fired at the window that it was coming from. I don't think they were firing at me at the time, but they might have done afterwards! So I emptied the bloody magazine at them, and the firing stopped. I don't know if I actually hit anyone, but it could have just frightened them away, so it did some good.

All over the beach there were dead bodies, and bits of bodies that hadn't been cleared up. The first wave had gone in at about eight o'clock and we landed at about half past nine or ten o'clock so there was still a lot of fighting around the beach. But we had been told not to stop for anything, just to get up the beach and keep going.

At the time there were landings going on all over the Normandy coast away to our right, but I wasn't aware of any of that at the time. I couldn't even tell you who was running beside me, you just had to go straight ahead, get up the beach, get onto dry land and into cover.

Then our major's fifteen hundredweight truck came up. The major said, 'Right, Kemp, you speak a bit of French. I want you to come with me.' We started driving through the German lines, and we had a Bren gun carrier supporting us. It was chaos; there was so much going on and so much noise. Bombs, shells and bullets flying everywhere – it was deafening.

And all the time you're wondering if you will be the next one. You lose yourself, you're not Clive Kemp, you're just an animal fighting for survival. The adrenaline was running through me, and I kept my gun ready all the time, although I didn't see anyone close enough to shoot again.

A friend of mine, a funny Yorkshireman called George Dransfield, was meant to be the driver of one of the trucks. But as he'd got off the landing craft, he'd twisted his ankle, and didn't think he could drive very well. So I drove instead. After just a short way we stopped in a village where there was an aid post. The major told him to get out of the truck and get himself cared for. But just as he crossed the road, *whup*! He was hit by a German sniper in a nearby church tower and died right there. I was really upset, but it had been drilled into us that we weren't allowed to stop, we had to get on, keep going, and get the bridge built. He was a member of my section of twenty blokes, someone I had known for years. I had eaten, trained and laughed with him.

We made our way across country towards the bridge, which was only a few miles inland. We couldn't stay on the roads because the Germans were defending them.

When we got to the village of Bénouville there was still some fighting going on, where the Paras were holding off the Germans. We arrived at almost exactly the same time as Lord Lovat and the commandos who had come to relieve the Paras. Although we didn't see the column coming in, I remember hearing the bagpipes as they approached. We had to go around the chateau to get to where we were headed, while they went straight to Pegasus Bridge. Some assault engineers had got there before us and taken off all the explosives that the Jerries had rigged to it, so we knew it was safe. That meant we'd have to prepare to build a second bridge a couple of hundred yards away, closer to Caen.

The first thing to do was to survey the ground where the bridge was going to be built. Some of the blokes jumped out of the truck to start doing that, while I lay on the ground with my gun, watching the road in case anything came down that way to attack us. There were lots of shells falling everywhere near the bridge, because the Germans were trying to knock it out. And the shells from our ships at sea were still flying over us at the Germans, and they were firing back over our heads at the ships. The noise was awful; it felt like hell on earth.

There was a big stone and cement works nearby on high ground, which the Germans were still occupying. It had a great big chimney, and they put an observer up that so they could see us clearly, and when they realised that we were going to build another bridge they shifted their fire onto us. We were vulnerable, because we had to get all our stuff out carefully to make it ready. You couldn't just dump it all around the place, everything had to be exactly where you needed it. So while we were doing that, they kept firing at us.

Once we'd prepared the ground, the sections had to be put together like a big Meccano set. It took six of us to carry each part – a big arched upright panel. This was then floated out onto pontoons, and the next bit was joined onto it with huge pins. You'd run back to get the next part, running all the time. And while we were at this, the Germans were lobbing mortars at us too. We had a system worked out between my section and the one working opposite us. You'd hear one coming in, and you'd shout, 'Right, drop!' and you'd all drop the big section at once and get flat. The problem was that the piece you were carrying wouldn't always stay upright, and could fall on you, so we had to work out how to avoid that too. We went like clockwork. You'd only stop if one went close, because the next one could get even closer. We had quite a few casualties there, but none of us actually died.

One of our officers was fighting mad. He had been in the Commandos, and decided he wanted some of the fighting that the Paras were doing. He was all for glory, really. He went off down one of the streets of Bénouville, after telling us he wanted to make sure it was safe down there. He had a sack full of grenades, and was chucking them through the windows. He'd only done a couple, near the bridge, and nine Germans came out and surrendered to him!

He told one of my mates to march them back to the rear, which he didn't bloody like – nine Jerries to march all the way back to the beaches! We saw them marching past with their hands on their heads. We looked at them, and we were all thinking, 'Their war's over, I wish mine bloody was!'

When you're in that situation, your adrenaline is going, it's like you're a bit mad. But we felt a bit sorry for them too; really they were just like us. In fact, they were middle-aged men who didn't have that much fight in them. I always remember the smell of their uniforms; they bloody stank, far worse than ours.

We ended up staying at Bénouville for six weeks, building the bridge and maintaining it. At first it was very difficult because even though we'd pushed the Germans back, their long-range guns could still reach us and they knew where the bridge was. They'd send fighter planes around too, attacking our pontoons. Every time they came over we'd scatter, run like hell. They hit the main bridge too, once with a bomb which didn't explode. You can still see the mark. Later they even started floating mines downstream, hoping they would hit our pontoons and blow them up. We had to try to stop them by using a motorboat with nets.

The bridge area was still front line for a long time, because our boys were trying to get the Germans out of Caen, where they had all their armour. When you were off duty you had to get underground, get under cover if you could. They sent over mortar shells and bombs all the time.

My billet was a hole in the ground, in the grounds of the chateau at Bénouville. It wasn't easy to keep yourself clean and tidy there. But I do remember going to get my hair cut. We had a bloke there who'd been a hairdresser in Civvy Street. And if you went to look for him and asked, 'Is the barber about?' he wouldn't answer you. You had to ask for the hairdresser! But he was very good. Anyway, one day I found him, and asked him if he would cut my hair. So there I was, sitting on a wooden box with this old cloth around my neck, when all of a sudden *brrrtttt!* a bloody German plane came over, firing at our bridge. And there's me, legging it to cover with this thing like a cloak flying out behind me, looking like Batman! Once it had gone I slunk back there with my tail between my legs. Of course it hadn't been firing at me, but I didn't know that at the time! All my mates laughed their bloody heads off at the sight of me running about with this hairdresser's cape around me. Mind you, they were flat on the floor too!

Another time I was on picket duty there. We all had to take turns. It was four in the morning, and I was curled up in my hole in the ground. We'd all dug one out for ourselves. It looked like a shallow grave, so you could roll yourself up in your blankets and a groundsheet. I'd found myself an old door too, which I could lay over the top of it. There was just a small space left for me to slide into it, so I could be nice and cosy. So anyway, four o'clock in the morning, and it was my turn to do the picket duty. I heard my mate outside call me: 'Kempy! It's your turn!' So I started to wriggle out of my little hole. And suddenly this bloody gun went off, one we'd never heard before; it was a German eighty-eight. Now the big guns usually go *BOOM! ... Wheee! ... BANG!* and you have a bit of time to take cover. But the eighty-eight just goes *SSHHHEEWW! CRACK!* and there's no time to move. Anyway, this thing went right close to me, and I jumped a mile. I banged my head against the wooden door and felt something warm and wet on the side of my head. Blood and pus was running down my face. 'Christ,' I thought, 'I've been hit!' Bloody hell, it hurt.

But I could still move all right, so I went and relieved the guard and did my two hours' duty. I had some breakfast, and told the officers that I had to go to the aid post, because I thought I'd been hit in my ear. The medical officer, a first lieutenant, was a proper little bastard. 'What's happened to you?' he asked. So I told him, and he didn't even look at me because I'd cleaned myself up a bit. And the bastard got out his pen with red ink, that's the one to show you're malingering, and wrote that on my records. I went to my major, and told him what had happened. I told him there hadn't been any wounded at the aid post, so I hadn't pushed my way in, and that the MO hadn't even looked at me properly. The major had a look at me, and told me to push my finger into my ear to see if it was still hurting. I did, and all this blood and stuff came out. So he put me in the jeep and ran me down to the aid post again. He tore the lieutenant off a strip, and told him to look at me properly. It turns out I'd had a massive boil in my ear, which had burst when the shell had gone off near me. So the red ink was rubbed off my record.

The chateau itself was full of French girls who were pregnant with German soldiers' babies. We were all called together by the officers and told to leave them well alone: many of them had VD and other diseases. 'Keep your flies done up!' they told us. But I felt sorry for them – they never had any soap or cigarettes, and I often went to give them some help.

Later in the war, when we were building a bridge near Paris, we saw some French people bullying some French women in the town square. They were shaving their heads, and beating them, because they had been friendly with the Germans. Some of our blokes went to try to stop them, but they turned their guns on us and told us to stay away as it was none of our business.

When we were off-duty, we could walk down the canal towpath, towards Pegasus Bridge. That's where the famous Café Gondrée is: the first building to be liberated in the whole of France. It was run by Monsieur and Madame Gondrée. They'd done some work for the Resistance, and hid a load of champagne in their garden. They dug it all up when the Paras landed! They were always open for us. And there were always two little tots playing about there, one of whom was Arlette Gondrée, who runs the café today.

I said in my schoolboy French, 'I've got some chocolate. Would it be all right if I bring it up next time I'm here, and give it to your daughters?'

'Ah, merci Monsieur!' they said to me, and so I turned up the next day with ten bars of the stuff! You see, I didn't smoke, and I used to swap the fags from my rations for chocolate. I'd usually eat it myself, but whenever there were kids about I'd always give it to them. Monsieur Gondrée called the little girls out, and explained to them that I was giving them nice things. They curtsied, and said, 'Thank you Monsieur Tommy!' which was their name for English soldiers. I can remember Arlette sitting on my knee, speaking a few English words.

Some years after the war a few of my platoon arranged a trip back to Bénouville for a couple of days, and we visited the café of course.

I asked Arlette whether she remembered the soldier who came to the café every evening, gave her chocolate and played with her, and yes, she said she did remember me, even though she had only been four years old. That was a wonderful moment, and we were both very emotional. She kissed me on both cheeks and was so pleased to see me.

Whenever I go back to Pegasus now, I always go to the café to see Madame Gondrée. She always invites me in to the back room, away from the other customers. I cry very easily, and sometimes I end up wishing I hadn't gone. I always visit George Dransfield's grave in the churchyard at Bénouville too, to put a cross on it.

Last year the visit was more difficult because I can't use my legs very well, but with a bit of help I managed to get over there and take part in a march across the bridge with other members of our Normandy Veterans Association. Unfortunately it was raining, but we went behind the Band of the Island of Jersey, which was a dream come true.

Sometimes when I go there I meet modern-day soldiers. They always ask me about what happened there, and make me feel so bloody proud. I never want to make myself out as a hero. The heroes are people like my mate, who are still over there, buried. I was just a bloke who had been trained to do a job, and did it well. I was with a great company, the best, who were chosen to do one of the most important jobs of D-Day.

Film still from the D-Day landings showing commandos aboard a landing craft on their approach to Sword Beach © IWM BU 1181

Commando troops coming ashore from LCIs (Landing Craft Infantry) © IWM B 5245

'This ship is similar to the one I landed on, and I had to wade ashore like this.'
© *IWM B 5092*

Getting the equipment needed ashore on Sword beach. 'This would have been later in the day after I landed.' ©IWM B 5116

Royal Marine Commandos attached to 3rd Division for the assault on Sword Beach move through Colleville-sur-Orne on their way to relieve forces at Pegasus Bridge. 'I remember hearing their bagpipes as they arrived.'
© IWM B 5067

Royal Engineers constructing a Bailey bridge

A heavily laden universal carrier crosses Pegasus Bridge
© *IWM B 5234*

Transport moving across the Caen Canal Bridge at Bénouville. The bridge was renamed Pegasus Bridge, after the mythical winged horse on the formation sign of British airborne forces. Note the glider next to the bridge in the background. 'This was taken opposite Café Gondrée. Our bridge was about a quarter of a mile to the right.'
© *IWM B 5288*

Chapter Nine

TO FALAISE

Caen was proving to be a thorn in the side of the Allied advance. The once-beautiful city, just a few miles south of Pegasus Bridge, was now a stronghold of German Panzer divisions, determined not to let it go without a fight. A series of attacks managed to encircle most of the city before Operation Goodwood was launched on 18 July 1944. As well as attacks by armoured groups and infantry, the operation has become best-known for its aerial bombardment. Hundreds of Allied aircraft bombed the German positions in and around Caen with high explosives, smashing some of their most important Panzer formations. It was a sight which no one who witnessed it could forget. For Clive, just a few miles away, it was an awe-inspiring sight; although with the inaccurate bombing techniques of the time it was dangerous for him too!

When the breakout finally happened, the Germans were sent on the run. But Hitler refused to countenance a full retreat, and ordered a counter-attack on the American forces at Mortain on 7 August.

When that inevitably failed, the last of his useful divisions were scattered or in full flight. Almost completely surrounded, they headed east towards the area known by the name of a town on its northern edge – Falaise. Falaise is about fifteen miles to the south-east of Caen, and all the SS and *Wehrmacht* troops retreating from the Cherbourg Peninsula and Normandy were forced into a small pocket there.

Attacked on all sides, the Germans tried desperately to keep an escape route open; this was in and around the village of Chambois on the eastern edge. They made many counter-attacks to try to keep the surrounding roads open, and many Allied units found themselves targeted by enemy fire as cut-off German forces tried to break out. During the battle, Clive's unit was stationed in and around the town of Vassy, south of Villers-Bocage, right in the path of the Germans retreating from the Cherbourg peninsula. He and his comrades were called on to be ready to defend themselves at short notice, even though they were unprepared.

Eventually, after some frantic fighting, the neck of the pocket was closed on 21 August. Fifty thousand German soldiers were trapped and captured. Thousands more were dead on the roads leading through the pocket, where they had been attacked relentlessly by the RAF with guns, rockets and bombs. The roads around Chambois were graveyards of men, trucks and tanks.

With the battle of the Falaise Gap over, the Allies could push ahead with the liberation of France. As they drove east, they found the Germans regrouping and ready to fight; many bridges had been destroyed to hold up the advance, and the 71st Field Company was always right at the front of the action, leaving Vassy on 23 August for Vernon.

While we were at the bridge, staying at Bénouville, the war was still going on. The Allies were trying to get through Caen, but the Jerries had all their armour there and we couldn't push past them.

I remember when they sent over hundreds of bombers to attack the Germans in Caen. The Yanks turned around as soon as the ack-ack came up, and dropped their bombs early. One stick landed just a couple of hundred yards from our position.

But the bombers flew over us for hours to attack the city. I remember when they started the Jerries were firing like mad from every direction, and our RAF boys flew right through it to make the attack. By the end of the evening, there was only one gun left firing. We thought it was a thousand-bomber raid, but we later found out it wasn't quite that many. They filled the sky.

The raid itself was terrible. We were about four miles from Caen, and the bloody ground was shaking, it was very frightening. Caen was flattened, and eventually we had to drive though it to get to where we had to build our next bridge. We needed a special bulldozer to go ahead to clear the road. It was worse than London during the Blitz, and I watched it all from the back of a lorry as we drove through. I remember seeing the old castle in the city, and that was still just about standing.

When Caen finally fell, they started chasing the Germans back to the Falaise gap as fast as they could. They were counter-attacking a lot, to try and keep the gap open. Our commanders thought they might come past us, where we were working. So they told us we all had to serve as infantry for a while.

I was a Bren gunner, even though I hadn't really used one since the invasion, when I shot at the window of that house. We dug in by the side of this road, getting ready to fight back if the retreating Germans came our way. We were all getting really nervous because we knew they were desperate to escape. Now if you have a weapon, you're supposed to keep it in proper working order. But I'd been so busy building bridges, filling in shell holes and making roads that I hadn't had time to look after my Bren properly. Anyway, I shoved a magazine into my gun, and the order came to test-fire our weapons. So I squeezed the trigger and ... nothing happened! I pulled the magazine out to see what was wrong, and found that everything had rusted, and it wouldn't fire! So I checked the next magazine – same thing! All four Brens on our section had the same problem. The only one which would work was one belonging to a bloke who used to stay at headquarters, so we put his in position up front. Luckily for us, the Germans never came.

Cromwell tanks moving across York Bridge, a Bailey bridge over the Caen Canal and the River Orne, during Operation Goodwood. 'My unit built 22 major bridges from Normandy to Germany and countless smaller ones.' ©IWM B 7656

Once that little scare was over it was back to our job of opening the way for the army. Our life was always a rush. If ever the tanks got held up, we had to be there, filling holes and making bridges, just so they could get through as fast as possible. We pushed them all the way across France, towards a place called Vernon.

There had been a lot of resistance there, and there were still bodies on the top of the old bridge. Some of our chaps had to go and get the bodies and give them a decent burial. There were German soldiers, and civilians too. The civilians were poor buggers, you couldn't tell them where they should go, they just wanted to get away. You'd see women with prams, who had just been trying to get away from the bombs and the bullets.

Some officers asked us to come down and help to fight, because our company had some light mortars, and I went because I was a Bren gunner. I spent most of my time sheltering under lorries feeling scared. I remember waking up one morning, crawling out from under the lorry, and just up the road I could see an abandoned pillbox which the Jerries had used to cover the road. I thought it would make a much nicer shelter for me, so I planned to sleep there that night. Sure enough, when I finished work it was pitch dark so I went up there with my blankets only to find someone had got there before me. I didn't mind though, and curled up next to him to keep warm. When I woke up, I found it was a bloody dead Jerry! I didn't fancy going back there again, because it would have been a load of work to drag him out and bury him. So we just left him there, trusting that someone would find him. You have to remember that I'd been at war for five years by then, so I wasn't so squeamish about dead soldiers. Civilians were another matter, they could make us very upset, we'd all be thinking of our own homes and families. We would often volunteer to help bury women and children. The children in particular upset me, and I would cry just to see them. I can still cry today just thinking about it.

I remember the first German I buried. He was by the side of a road which had been attacked and I was asked to bury him. Now all along the side of the road were what we used to call 'funk holes', little holes where you could shelter if you were being fired on. So I said to my mate, 'Just lie him across this hole,' and I thought I'd get him into it by jumping on his tummy. The hole was about five and a half feet across, and he was about six feet tall. I know this sounds terrible now, but you must remember, it was war, he was German and I was British. So anyway I jumped on him to try to get him into this hole, and *brraaaaghhhh!* he moaned really loudly as I knocked the air out of his body. Scared me to death, and I never did that again!

Sometimes one of your own men would get killed while you were building a bridge, but you couldn't stop working. They would get his body out of the way, and sometimes you wouldn't know about it until you knocked off at the end of your shift. We used to make a joke about it: 'Tommy Smith got hit today.'

'Oh good, did they take his head off?'

We weren't very nice about it, but that's how we dealt with the loss.

Human bodies weren't the only ones we had to worry about. The smell I most remember from being in France was that of the dead cattle. Like Jersey, Normandy was full of dairy farms, and hundreds of cattle were out in the fields during the fighting and bombing. So many of them died, and of course they started to stink really badly. It always came down to us engineers, as usual, to either blow them up or bury them. That was a hell of a job with just pick and shovel.

The other strong smell I remember from the war is the stink of German uniforms. All of them smelt horrible – I think they must have been treated with something. You could smell them from miles away. I think ours had been treated too, against gas, but they didn't smell so badly.

Anyway, the bridge at Vernon had been bombed really badly, and there were craters everywhere. All the buildings nearby had been smashed to bits, so there was lots for us to do. First we had to get a road built to the place where we were going to build the bridge, so we could get all our heavy equipment there. We were there for about four weeks because there was so much to do, with building extra roads and repairs.

All through those four weeks we were being shelled. The Germans were retreating, and they didn't want the Allies to be following them, so they were trying to cut our bridge off. It was noisy all the time, with the noise of our building work, the shelling, German planes coming over with bombs, and our own planes getting after them. We could tell the difference between a German plane and one of ours, so we knew when we had to get out of the way.

Personally, I never ran from a plane. When we were retreating to Dunkirk, an older bloke told me, 'Don't run, because you'll be running into trouble. The best thing is to just lie flat. If something lands ten yards away, the debris will all go over you; and if it's a direct hit, you won't need to worry about it!' So every time we had an air attack I'd just get down as flat as I could, and I got away with it. I did see blokes trying to run away, and they just ran into where the trouble was and got hurt. I was lucky.

We worked so hard on that bridge, flat out with hardly any rest. The rations would be brought up and half a dozen of us at a time would be able to scoff it as fast as we could, then it would be back to work. The food was always awful. We would usually get some kind of stew, God knows what it was, and it was usually cold by the time it got to us. Sometimes we would be able to warm it up if we had time to make a fire, but usually we just had to get it down fast and get back to it. We always envied the Americans, they ate better then than we do nowadays. They had something new every day, and plenty of it, and how we hated their guts! They had twice as much as us, they ate better, they lived better, their uniform was better, their equipment was better. Where we had to use a pick and shovel, they had big mechanical diggers come to do the job.

At Vernon we stayed in some of the derelict houses, although that was dodgy because the Germans used to booby-trap them. Personally I never saw one, but we were always being told of people opening doors and being blown up, so we were always careful.

I would still rather have been in a derelict house or a bunker than in a tank. I could never have been in a tank. I can remember seeing some of ours get blown up; Shermans were the worst, they used to call them Ronsons because, like the famous lighters, they went up every time. We'd seen into those tanks after a battle and seen the remains of the crews; just puddles of fat left in the well of the tank. But every time we built a bridge and saw the tanks going across towards the fighting, the blokes on board would say they were quite happy with steel all around them, and would never swap their jobs for ours! The army is funny like that, everybody thinks their job is the best or the safest. I wouldn't have had their job for all the tea in China.

I did get to drive one in Normandy, though, when some were being serviced near us. I got in with the commander, and they battened down all the hatches. I hated it. I used to see so many tank commanders hit by snipers because they used to roll along without the top hatch closed. Blown-up tanks were terrible to see, especially if there had been a big battle like there was at Argentan. We went through that.

Aeroplanes were the same. I met quite a few pilots who used to boast that they would be asleep in a nice comfy bed every night, and have a nice breakfast before going off to 'work'. But I saw quite a few planes which had been shot down or crashed, with the burned bodies of the pilots inside, and I couldn't envy them any more.

Left: Sherman tanks crossing a Bailey bridge over the Seine at Vernon
© IWM B 9750

Below: An ambulance and infantry crossing the River Seine at Vernon © IWM BU 185

Chapter Ten

TOWARDS GERMANY

After the German collapse at Falaise, the Allies pushed ahead towards Germany. But it would be a long time before they could cross the Rhine and get into the enemy's own country. Many rivers and canals had been mined, and their bridges destroyed, to hold up the Allied armour.

The 71st Field Company was at the front of the advance, ready to lay its bridges whenever necessary. The bridge at Vernon, west of Paris, was 642 feet long, and Clive spent four weeks building and maintaining it under constant fire.

Pushing ahead towards Belgium, he experienced some of the better aspects of the war; liberating French towns, kissing French girls, and enjoying the food and drink pressed on him by grateful French citizens.

As they got closer to Germany though, resistance stiffened. Hitler knew that he had to slow the advance before the Allies crossed the border. Bridges were blown, ruins were booby-trapped and roads were mined. Clive and his companions would have to cope with all these dangers, as well as doing the job they were there for.

The Albert canal in Belgium was a difficult place to be, and Clive was involved in battles where he fired his Bren gun in anger. He knows he killed people. The first time, he went to see their bodies. He never did it again, though, and the memory still brings tears to his eyes.

By now the members of Clive's company were seasoned veterans, getting used to the awful sights and smells of war. They were expert at bridge building, to the extent that they were used to train other units.

But despite their experience, some inevitably became casualties. Clive still remembers his friends being hit, and how they used to deal with the shock by making a joke out of it. Eventually his own luck ran out too.

One place that got very hot was in Belgium, near where the First World War battlefields were, when we were bridging the Albert canal.

I had gone over to the other side of the canal with my mate, on a patrol. Our company was building the bridge, and our job was to keep the area safe so they could do the work. We were walking down the towpath, and I had my Bren gun with me, when we saw this Jerry with a white flag coming towards us. Now we'd been told not to mess about, and if we weren't sure they were genuine, to shoot them. My mate was saying, 'Don't take any prisoners, shoot the bastards!'

So I was just getting ready to let them have it with my gun when I saw it was a Red Cross flag. Another minute and I would have let them have it, cut the bloody lot down. It was some Jerries bringing in some wounded, Tommies as well as their own. Our officer told me I had to take them back to behind our lines, and we had to ferry them across to our side in our little boat.

So we got on with ferrying them over, and at one point I had to take three Germans at once. We hurried them on, and I noticed that one of them had his boot in his hand, with his foot still in it! But we made the buggers do the rowing anyway.

I really can't imagine myself being so vicious normally. But when the adrenaline is going, and there's all that banging and shooting going on, your mind is just against them. I'm not that sort of bloke really, I am very sentimental, and I can't imagine the sort of bloke I was then. When action started I think I was vicious. I'd shoot at anything that moved, whatever it was. I was so strongly against the Germans.

In our company we wouldn't usually take prisoners, because for every one you took, two of you had to look after him. If there was fighting going on, even if somebody might have been trying to surrender, you couldn't take a chance because they could turn on you. Much better to shoot the bastards. If you saw soldiers coming towards you, you'd let go with the Bren gun, thirty bullets coming out really quick; you were bound to hit something. But after the first time I did that, I never went to look at what I'd hit. I didn't want to know the mess I'd made of someone. And you'd carry on fighting, scared, even if your mates were hit. We were always told to keep going, not to stop, because you had a bridge to build. Somebody else would take their place. After the firing died away, you'd feel the madness leaving you, and the real you came back again slowly. You'd chat about your mates who had been wounded or killed, but you couldn't dwell on it because you were so busy. It shook you up, but you had to carry on.

Today, I feel awful that I killed people, in any of the battles I was in. I'm a gentle person who doesn't like fighting at all. But when the firing started you had to remember it was either them or you, and you were fighting to stay alive. You were a different man.

Another problem was that as we pushed across the country, the French just didn't want us there. In the big cities it was different, but in the country they weren't happy to see us at all. They didn't want our big lorries and tanks digging up their fields and all the fighting smashing up their farms. I saw a bulldozer tank knock down buildings on narrow streets so the big transporters could get through – just demolishing people's homes. They weren't going to be friendly, were they?

In the towns and cities it was different because they weren't usually so damaged. We'd be going around the bars and restaurants when we had a bit of time off, spending our money, and they liked that. I never met a really friendly Frenchman though.

We didn't always have it our own way, even though the advance was quite fast once we got out of Normandy. The Germans counter-attacked when we were in Belgium, and for a few days we were surrounded. The food couldn't get through, and we had nothing. I remember very clearly finding a loaf of bread in a ditch. It was a brown loaf, covered in mildew. But we were hungry, so I scraped the mould off, gave some to my mates, and ate it anyway. But not long afterwards we broke out and were on the move again.

I must say Anderlecht was great. We arrived there just after it had been liberated, and the people were all going crazy. At that time in my life I was known for not being a drinker; I never joined in with all the drunken behaviour of my mates. But in Anderlecht I was drunk for four days. The locals were really nice to us there, and looked after us very well. They always invited us to stay at their houses, and made us feel like we'd done something good.

While we were there, we were close to the Siemens factory. They made these nice torches there, ones which didn't need batteries because you squeezed a handle which worked a dynamo to make the light come on. So we went to the factory and asked if we could have some, but they wouldn't let us have any! Instead I went asking about, and a nice bloke went home and got me one from there. I swapped it with him for a couple of packets of fags.

A funny thing happened in Anderlecht though, something which landed me in trouble. I had written to my wife back home, telling her not to worry about me. I explained that all our letters were censored, so I couldn't tell her where I was. But not to worry, I said, even though my work was dangerous I was fine and being careful.

Anyway, she went to the pictures with her friend, and they had the Movitone news on before the main film, like they used to in those days. And what does she see on the news but Clive, with four girls on each arm, tipsy, walking up the main street of Anderlecht! She wrote me a letter saying that she could see I was in no danger at all, but was enjoying myself! I was only repaying the ladies' hospitality ...

When we came to Brussels they had asked for us engineering boys to go through it with the tanks, sitting on top of them. They thought the Jerries might have put obstacles in our way through the city. That was bloody uncomfortable, sitting on a great lumbering tank, with all the fumes coming off the engine. Our faces turned black from them. The crew would sometimes poke their heads out of the hatches and laugh at us, so we'd give them the old two-fingered salute and a raspberry! The people were going mad, which cheered us up. They were throwing flowers and everything at us. But once we got through there we had to get back on our trucks, and in the back of a truck you can only see back to where you've been, not what's coming.

While we were there, we saw the local police being bloody horrible. These poor local people were coming up to us asking for cigarettes, and the police were using their batons to clear them out of the way, they were being really nasty. We had to throw our fags to the people away from the police, so they could actually get them.

But it was great to feel like liberators for a while. The girls were going out of their way to kiss you, people were giving us food we knew they couldn't afford – they loved us there. It was lovely to think we had got through to them.

By this time, we were all getting quite battle-worn, as we'd pushed all the way across France. We hadn't had much respite; all these concerts by Vera Lynn and people like that never happened for us, we were always just flat out working. Once or twice someone might have come to play the piano with a couple of girls in short skirts, but they'd get annoyed when we started singing along, singing our heads off. We were typical British, nothing got us down and we would just keep going. We were never told about having to go to the last man; we were always ready to work bloody hard. We lived the life of the nomad. Whenever we had a break we would scrape a hole in the ground, spread out our two thin blankets, and sleep if we could. I was always careful where I dug in. I saw men who had dug in close to roads get crushed by lorries or tanks going past in the middle of the night. Clive always used his head! I always looked for a prime place, to make sure I was safe, warm and dry.

One of the things to look forward to were letters from home. The delivery would come, and you'd listen for you name. 'Kemp!' and there would be something for you. Sometimes you'd get parcels. My wife used to make marzipan for me, because I loved that. I'd get it from the parcel, then hide it and eat it in the dark at night. I had to share some of it, but when you're sharing with twenty blokes it doesn't last long. So when they asked me what I'd got in the parcel, I'd always say socks, or something like that.

We were close though. The phrase 'band of brothers' is a good one, because that's how you had to be. We'd read our letters out loud to each other, although I'd always leave out the spicy bits of mine. It was good to hear news of home, and you'd share, and that made our camaraderie stronger. Every now and again I'd get a Red Cross message back from mum and dad in Jersey, and my wife in England.

We played cards too, and you could owe thousands of pounds, but nobody cared. I loved cards. We'd play Nap, which I loved, or Brag, which I didn't. I couldn't bluff well enough – my face always used to give me away! Pontoon was another favourite. In fact, the day before I went on leave to get married, I had about forty quid in my pocket for the celebrations, and I got involved in a card school and lost the lot! I had to tell my wife someone had pinched it.

Every now and again someone would have a football and if there was a spare moment, which was rare, we would have a kick around. You could never make a proper fixture list though, because everything was moving so quickly. I used to love watching more than playing, and would always volunteer to be the spare man. They were never very skilful games, we were all in big hobnail army boots on lumpy fields, but we had fun.

My best mate through all of this was Stan Sharman. When you're in a platoon of thirty-odd blokes, you tend to latch on to someone to be around. He was a lot like me. He wasn't a rowdy, show-off type of bloke. In fact, if anything, I was the more boisterous one. I always liked to be able to have a laugh, to be able to take the mickey out of someone.

It's always good to know your mate is close by when the bombs start to fall; you can look after each other. I always used to tell him what I'd learned at Dunkirk, after seeing so many men killed when they tried to run away from enemy aeroplanes: 'Don't run'. I never ran away, just dropped flat with my arms over my head. I'd lay flat, almost stop breathing, waiting until they'd gone. That way there had to be a direct hit to get you. I knew they weren't after us anyway; they were after the bridge. Quite a few of the blokes had asked me about Dunkirk, and we'd had meetings about it where I passed on whatever advice I could. I told them if there was an attack while you were in a vehicle, just get out, get into a ditch, and stay down; again, they weren't after you in particular, they wanted the vehicles.

After we left the fun and games in Anderlecht and Brussels, we had to pay for all the parties with some very hard work, and it was around this time that I had one of my worst experiences. I was on mine-detecting duty. We often had to go out clearing mines if the sappers weren't there to do it. The problem was, we had to clear a space for all our bridging equipment, and make sure the riverbank and the roads to it were safe and clear.

The way we did it was to work in threes. One bloke would go at the front with the mine detector. You'd be wearing earphones, sweeping the detector over the ground, listening carefully. Any time it went over something metal, it would whistle in your ears. The problem was, you didn't know if it was a mine or just a bit of shrapnel. The next bloke had to mark what you'd found, then the one behind him had to use whatever tool he had to lift it out of the ground. Being the one with the detector was particularly nerve-wracking, and you'd take it in turns. You'd be all of a shake, not knowing what was underneath you. Twenty minutes of detecting, and your nerves would be in bits. Then you'd move back to be the one lifting, and the marker would move up to take the detector. Meanwhile, other chaps would be marking where you had gone by running out lengths of white tape. That would show everyone where it was clear. Unfortunately I saw a number of people needlessly killed doing this, as they wandered over to where the tape was across an uncleared area, getting themselves blown up. People were also killed because the detectors had missed mines.

This one day, I was the one at the back, lifting whatever the one with the detector had found. Suddenly, the bloke ahead of me, who had just changed from lifting to marking, knelt on one of the bloody things. Of course it went up, a huge bang. Luckily I was a couple of metres behind him, kneeling down. I was blown over backwards. Somehow all the shrapnel missed me, but all this muck had been blown into my eyes; some of it was the remains of the poor bloke who'd knelt on the mine. I couldn't see a bloody thing. I thought I was blind, blind for life. My face was hurting like hell and I thought I was going to die. All these thoughts were running through my head, so fast. I was shouting to everyone, 'Please, wash my eyes out!' They managed to get me out of the place to the medical tent, but in the field there they couldn't do anything to help me. Luckily there was an airfield nearby, and they put me on a jeep to get there. Then they got me on a plane to Brussels where there was a proper hospital. All I can remember of that journey was holding these rags up to my eyes, thinking I was blind so young.

When I got to Brussels they operated on me to remove all the muck that was in my eyes, and said they'd even popped my eyeballs out of their sockets to clean them properly. I remember opening my eyes and seeing light again for the first time when they took the bandages off. It was still a bit blurry but I didn't care; I just knew I could see again. For a few days it was as if I was crying all the time, but it gradually got better and I got back to my mates. I found out what had happened to the other blokes who had been on the mine duty with me. The one who'd knelt on the mine had just been blown to bits; he was dead pretty much straight away. But the one in front of him, who had been holding the detector, had been very lucky. The blast had thrown him forward, and he had fallen down, rolling to one side. The reason he was lucky was that if he'd fallen the other way he would have landed on another mine and blown himself up.

An M10 tank destroyer crossing a Bailey bridge over the Albert canal in Belgium,
11 September 1944 © IWM BU 842

Chapter Eleven

A BRIDGE TOO FAR

The push through France and Belgium had been tough for the 71st Field Company. It had lost men and materiel, and its soldiers were battle-weary. Clive, who soon recovered from the damage to his eyes from the exploding mine, was soon to be a distant part of one of the next major efforts of the war – Operation Market Garden, known to many from the title of the book and film *A Bridge Too Far*.

The Allied strategy thus far had been to move towards Germany on a broad front, but General Montgomery's plan was for a fast, narrow thrust across some essential bridges to outflank the enemy from the north. The main part of the attack on 17 September 1944 was made by parachutists, some of them veterans of Pegasus Bridge. They dropped near the bridges which crossed several important waterways, including the Maas and the Waal. Battles such as those at Nijmegen and Arnhem, where the Paras and American airborne troops fought so valiantly, have passed into folklore.

Together with thousands of other men, Clive was pushed towards the front of the advance which was meant to relieve the Paras and open the way into Germany. His engineers were hugely important to the plan.

But a series of failures meant that the operation didn't achieve what Montgomery had hoped. Speed was of the essence, as the men at Arnhem had limited ammunition and no heavy weapons.

All of the bridges had to be held, and repaired if they were destroyed. The problems came fast; radios didn't work properly, reinforcements didn't arrive, traffic clogged the narrow roads, and slowly the Paras were ground down by German armoured troops arriving from the east. Clive and his comrades could see and hear the battles as the Allies tried to batter a way through, but ultimately Monty's plan proved too ambitious. The remaining Paras at Arnhem, the 'bridge too far', were captured after heroic defence, and the Allies would have to find another way to get into Germany.

They would have to cross other rivers to do it, and the 71st was soon pressed into action elsewhere. They were involved in bridge defence and ferrying men and supplies at Nijmegen at the end of September, then went through Eindhoven on 30 September, and built six more bridges on their way to the Maas at Gennep, where they arrived in February 1945. The bridge at Gennep was more than four thousand feet long, by far their longest. Soon after that they built one at Venlo, over the River Maas again. This bridge was opened by General Dempsey, the Commander-in-Chief of the Second Army. He told the weary sappers that it was over this bridge that the heavy weapons for the Battle of Germany would flow. The end was in sight for the Allies, but for the Germans there were many bloody battles still to be fought.

The company's first bridge over the Rhine was at Xanten. Started on 24 March, it was a quarter of the length of the bridge at Gennep. But because it represented the first incursion into their homeland, the Germans were determined to stop it being built.

When the Paras landed at Arnhem, they were pushed forward as fast as they could. They thought that if the operation succeeded, we might be needed to replace any bridges that were blown by the Germans.

The problem was that it didn't go as it should have, and while the fighting was going on, we were stuck just a little way behind the lines with all our gear in a traffic jam, trying to get through. There was so much stuff on the roads that not even the tanks could get through. It was one giant balls-up. I think Montgomery had the right idea, but the Germans fought well and things didn't work out.

I remember watching the planes flying over us, and further ahead you could see things dropping out of them as they tried to reinforce and resupply the bridgeheads.

The idea was that the Paras would take the bridges and open them up for the rest of us to come through, make any repairs and make sure the rest of the army could cross over into Germany.

But the Jerries fought really hard, and the bridges weren't taken.

The Germans had the road we were on zeroed for their artillery just a little way ahead of where we were, so it was really difficult to get forward. I remember some tanks managing to get off the road and towards the action. We were stuck there for days, not knowing what was happening. The ordinary soldier is always in the dark, and no one told us anything. The Paras just got killed or captured. It really was a 'bridge too far'.

At one point we were heading towards a place where we'd been told to look for a good site to make a bridge, and make a road to link up to it. But the whole area was mined, and there were white tapes marking out where you shouldn't go. These cocky commandos turned up, green berets, tough as hell. They were walking along a place where there wasn't any tape. They were heading to this posh house by the river, to do a bit of looting. We said, 'Look, we haven't cleared beyond where the tapes are. Don't be bloody idiots, just leave it!' But they didn't want to know. They walked about ten yards, and *boom*! *boom*! Both of them were dead. Two young blokes, killed in action: looting action. The problem with some of these soldiers was that they thought they were so tough nothing could hurt them. They were commandos, trained to kill people with knives, that sort of thing. It went to their heads, and it got them killed. We'd gone through that stage, although not so much. I saw quite a few chaps killed because they didn't observe the white tapes.

Soon after that, we were busy preparing a road towards a bridging site. You had to get the road in place before the bridge could be used. The site for the road had been cleared of mines, and there were white tapes hanging from pickets marking where it was safe. As usual, the other side of the tapes was forbidden territory because we didn't know if there were more mines there. The major in charge came up to see how it was all getting on, in a half track with his driver at the wheel. When the officer had seen all he wanted to, the driver decided that he wouldn't reverse back the way he had come, but would try to turn around. The problem was, these half tracks have a big turning circle. He was leaning over the side of the door, looking backwards to see how far he could go, and he went over the tapes and suddenly whoosh! He went over a mine and it blew up right next to him. It took his head clean off. Another needless death.

Eventually we ended up moving into the area of Eindhoven and Nijmegen, where you could see there had been a lot of fighting. Buildings were ruined, there were some bodies which still hadn't been buried – all the usual destruction of war. But because we had seen it all before we didn't really notice. Once the Allies had pushed through and the advance caught up, we were on the move again.

One of the longest bridges we built was at Gennep. The Germans had flooded the area, which was quite low-lying. Nothing could get through, so it was really slowing the advance up. We pushed out the pontoons as fast as we could, but it took days and was really hard work. We were under fire all the time. We would lose blokes here and there to the attacks, but we had to keep working. It was endless. The hardest part of it was actually getting the stuff to the bridgehead. Then we were moving on, into Germany itself.

The first bridge we built there was at Xanten, over the Rhine. It was a very big one, more than a thousand feet across. We were under heavy fire the whole time because it was the tanks' way into Germany. Before we even started the British had been shelling the opposite bank for days beforehand, trying to soften up the resistance there so we could get on with our work without too much trouble. But the Germans always seemed to have something to fire back with. The noise of our shells going over, and theirs coming back, with the explosions all the time, was tremendous. It made our job very dangerous, and we always had an ear open for the next shell.

At that time my job was as a motorboat driver. I'd volunteered for it, of course. I would be the one who would help to guide all the parts of the bridge into place as they were floated out onto the river. I loved the challenge of that, you had to be very exact in the way you dealt with the current and everything. Anyway, one time I was waiting for the next piece to be ready, just waiting by the bank, when this officer came over to me; I think he was a brigadier. He was wearing one of those leather jerkins so I couldn't see his rank badges properly. He asked me if I would take him across to the other side. Of course he wasn't asking me, he was telling me – I had to take him. So I said, 'Yes, sir!' He waited until there was a lull in the shelling, and off we went. Now me and my mates had been there for a few days, and we knew what the different shells sounded like; which were ours, which were theirs, and which might fall close to us. We also knew when we didn't need to worry.

So there we were, part-way across, when a whole load of shells started coming over from the Jerries, making a big noise as they headed into our positions on the bank. And this brigadier started shouting, 'Turn back, turn back Sapper!' because he had the wind up him. And I turned round to him and said, 'Not f***ing likely!' because I knew we'd be safer where we were going.

I put my foot down and got us over there as fast as possible. When we got there he said, 'That was good thinking, Sapper!' I told him we knew the sounds of all the guns and what was likely to cause us trouble.

Now about a month later, a Military Medal was sent to us, to be awarded to the motorboat section. I'm sure it was meant for me. The problem was, this brigadier hadn't asked my name, so the sergeant in charge of the transport section kept it, didn't he!

It would have been nice to have had that medal, although army blokes often had a laugh about them. They reckon that anyone with a Victoria Cross was either a very brave idiot, or drunk. And the bloke who sorted our mail got an MM too!

Having said that, I often got myself into trouble by volunteering to do difficult things. They'd ask for men to go out at night where we wanted to build a bridge, to check the site over, and I always had my hand up. The others thought I was bloody mad.

One of the other things I volunteered to do was ride a motorbike.

One of our dispatch riders had been injured or something, and a notice appeared at our headquarters asking for someone to take over. So guess who put his name down! I went to see the Motor Division officer. 'OK, Kemp.' he said, and that was it. I hadn't really ridden a proper motorbike before, only decrepit old things, but as always I was keen to learn something new. How difficult could it be? You just get on and keep your eyes about you.

The job involved taking orders and instructions from one company t another, and sometimes ferrying people about too. The other important thing we had to do was to go ahead of the company when it was on the move, to scout for billets where we could all stay. The dispatch riders always did that in twos. We had to look for something like a school hall or a big farm, where everyone could fit. It wasn't usually too difficult, because along the main roads in particular, everyone had evacuated, there were hardly any Germans about. You could just move right in. Sometimes we even went into a church. Good, solid stone buildings were the best.

It was always good fun; you had a lot more independence and could be your own person. If you were going somewhere you could always stop on the way back for a break somewhere. And of course you looked good. You had these nice leather trousers and big boots.

Once though, we drove up to the gates of a place which looked quite promising at first. There were loads of stone buildings, and plenty of huts where we could have put our blokes. I thought it was probably a tannery, because it absolutely stank. We'd stayed in tanneries before, like the one at Porlock, but the closer we got, the worse the smell got, until we decided we couldn't stay there. It really was horrible. We got as far as the gates, but never actually went in. We went on and found somewhere else instead. Later we found out why it had been so terrible. It was Belsen.

Eventually, as we got further into Germany, my career as a dispatch rider came to a sudden end. I was riding along in the dark with the other bloke beside me when all of a sudden the road disappeared. I flew through the air and landed with an almighty crash, smashing the bike up and bashing myself up a bit too. Turns out the road had been shelled and I had driven right into a great big crater! When I came to, I decided that I'd had enough of motorbikes, and I asked for my old job back!

When we finished at Xanten some of us were sent along the river to help the Canadians, who were having problems getting their bridge across; I got posted even further along to help the Yanks. After all the training and bridge-building under fire that we'd done, they valued our experience.

We had to keep our wits about us when we first got into Germany, There was no time to be going out and about, and we were warned about booby traps and other ways the Jerries could get back at us. We were always warned not to go looting, because you never knew what might have been left to catch you out.

We found that when we were pushing at a very difficult spot, they would throw in their best troops, like the SS or more experienced *Wehrmacht* units. The worst were the Hitler Youth. When we captured them they would just spit in your face, they were pure Nazis. But when things were quiet their soldiers were not quite so fanatical.

One devious thing they used to do was to hide up trees as snipers. What they made these poor buggers do, although I'm sure many of them were volunteers, was strap themselves into the treetops. They would let the main infantry force go through, and wait until the engineers and other units came up. Then they would shoot at anything that moved.

That could hold us up for days, which would mean that the tanks couldn't get past on the bridges we had to build. They would radio to us, and tell us what was happening. Being engineers, they always wanted us to take care of it. The only way to get them would be to blow the tree down, because you couldn't see where they were. Even if you could, you didn't want to give your position away.

Now I was quite a fast, small bloke. I used to be 'volunteered' to take them out. You'd have to take a sort of Bangalore Torpedo, a long sausage of explosives, and wrap it around the base of the tree. You'd have to work out what his angles of fire were, so you could quickly make an approach from behind him where he couldn't get you very easily. It was like a game of cops and robbers. Once you'd put the explosives around the tree you'd leg it away before it blew up and took the tree down. You'd have to hope there wasn't another one waiting for you around the corner. It was really dangerous, but I was young at the time and took risks. It was an important job to do, and we had to get rid of them. You also had to do what you were told, even though you were frightened. Anyone who says they weren't frightened is a bloody liar. I was so lucky to get away with things like this. Mind you, today they say that if you step in dog mess it's good luck; I had fallen in a whole pit of the stuff in 1940 so maybe I had a lifetime's supply of it!

After Xanten there was a great big push to get across Germany, and we were kept busy building lots of smaller bridges. We had no idea how long we were going to be there, or where we were going. We didn't know about the Russians coming across Germany from the other side. The British soldier was only concerned with his own lot.

The push across the Elbe was very hard. The company was working hard to put a bridge across at Artlenburg, and me and quite a few of the rest of us were taken across to the German side to patrol and keep the banks clear. I remember this one time the food had arrived, and I went off to eat it. That meant a cold mess tin full of horrible stew, sitting on a bit of wreckage, nothing glamorous! As I was finishing, the officer came up to me and said he had about two hundred prisoners who had to go back to the rear. He said that since I had a Bren gun, I had to take them back! I was really worried about this. Even though they'd been disarmed, there was only me to look after them, and I wanted to steer clear. Every now and then I fired a shot into the air just to keep them in order. I got them back to where they were meant to go bloody quick, and headed back to my mates as fast as I could.

As we progressed we did notice that the calibre of the German soldiers start to change, until they were all either old men or young boys. It was quite a sorry picture really; we were well-equipped and our uniforms were in good nick, although not as nice as the Americans'. But the Germans were in rags; some of them had no boots on their feet. Officers always did better though. German officers were better dressed and better fed.

But they all suffered in the end. I can remember you'd see thousands and thousands of them in a line coming towards you, surrendering. They would march across the bridges that we had built. Where they went, where they put them, I just don't know. We'd be on the side of the road, and would have to stop work as they marched by. They would always be asking for cigarettes, and I'd always chuck them some, poor bastards. The state they were in, I felt sorry for them. You know, when Hitler had been in power, there were thousands and thousands of them with their arms in the air, 'Sieg Heil!' and all that. Where did they all go? We used to ask them, and they all replied, 'No, nichts Nazi, nichts Nazi.' We used to do the 'Heil Hitler' salute, and they'd do it back to us! We'd take the mickey out of them, with proper British army humour.

Funnily enough, after the war I had a good mate that I used to play snooker with. He'd been stationed in Germany, and had married a really lovely German girl. They lived next door to my brother. I went round there for dinner one time, and conversation turned to the war. We were talking about it for a while and I said, 'Bloody Germans. They all had their arms up saluting when Hitler was in power, but none of them wanted to know once he was beaten.' And she told me how it had been. (She spoke better English than me!) She said, 'We had to do it. We weren't really Hitlerites, we were just taught it from school. If you didn't do it you were an outcast, you could even be shot. You had no choice.'

But we did find that we could get on with the normal Germans. We'd make sure we had something to trade, and the women would take our washing in for us. In the end, they were just like us: families, missing their fathers and sons. We would take our washing, with a bit of soap, to the Frauleins, and they would be like our mothers, washing our stuff and looking after us. Sometimes you could pinch something from the cookhouse to give them to help them out.

Artlenburg was a fairly big bridge; it turned out to be the last we would build under fire.

When we had finished building the Venlo bridge, General Dempsey came and opened it officially. He cut the tape and told us we had done a good job. The usual bloody bullshit – he was there a long time after the firing had finished. That was always the way when there was a visit from the top brass; we had to waste a load of time and effort cleaning our equipment and our uniforms and boots, even though we knew they were just going to walk past us. We had better things to do than see them! I think that was most people's opinion.

Montgomery inspected us once. I remember he stopped to talk to a bloke a couple down the line from me. And the bloke told him a couple of home truths about the food and that sort of thing. And Monty turned to his aide and asked him to write it down. Nothing happened about it though, as usual. You could complain to an orderly officer and nothing would be done. In fact many of them could see you as a troublemaker.

17 September 1944: British Paratroops of 1st (British) Airborne Division give the 'V'-sign and 'thumbs up' inside one of the C-47 transport aircraft © IWM K 7570

Nijmegen and Grave 17–20 September 1944: An aerial view of the bridge across the Waal River at Nijmegen © IWM NYP 39728

Nijmegen and Grave 17–20 September 1944: Men and supplies drop from transport planes above Nijmegen. 'I could see drops like this but often in the wrong place.' IWM EA 38796

Men of HQ Troop of 1st Airlanding Brigade's Reconnaissance Squadron at Wolfheze on the outskirts of Arnhem, 18 September 1944. The man on the left is manning a PIAT. 'We were trying to get there quickly but were held up by narrow roads and logistical problems as well as heavy German resistance.' © IWM BU 1144

Another smashed bridge and our new one is in the background

Above: Venlo, over the River Maas. This bridge was opened by General Dempsey, the Commander-in-Chief of the Second Army. I am fourth on the right.

Left: Field Marshal Montgomery and senior officers cross a Bailey bridge over the Maas at Berg, 3 December 1944 © IWM B 12419

Chapter Twelve

SURRENDER

For the weary men building the bridges, firing the guns and driving the tanks, the days passed in a blur of hard work. They knew they were in Germany, but didn't know just how close the country was to surrender. Pockets of resistance still fought on, especially the Hitler Youth and SS detachments. As the Allies closed in from the west, Stalin's masses of tanks, men and women streamed across the country from the east.

As the ring tightened around Berlin, Hitler ordered no surrender and barricaded himself into his bunker. Children armed with bazookas took on tanks in the rubble of the city, already in ruins after the Allied bombing offensive.

Finally, surrounded, and with the Russians just yards from his hideout, on 30 April 1945 Hitler took his own life. On 4 May the Germans surrendered in the west, bringing the war in Europe to an end.

Needless to say, Clive and his mates were ready to celebrate!

But in the immediate aftermath, there was a lot of work to be done. German towns and cities had been ravaged by the bombings of the RAF and USAAF, and by the shells and bullets of the land war. Its roads were full of potholes, its bridges often shattered. People had lost their homes and jobs. The victorious Allies had learned a bitter lesson after the First World War, when they had imposed harsh penalties on Germany. That had inspired resentment, which had been fuel to the fire of Nazism.

This time they stayed in order to try and make good some of the damage; this would also mean that the occupying armies would be able to move around quickly and easily.

Of course, as engineers, Clive and his comrades were much in demand.

In the meantime, in Jersey, the Germans, along with the civilian population, had endured a time of starvation after the Normandy invasion. Supplies were cut off, and the garrison had quickly realised it was trapped. Any remaining food was quickly used up, and even the basics were running out as the cold winter of 1944 wore on. The visit of the Red Cross ship SS *Vega* in December brought some relief, but life remained hard for everyone, including Clive's adoptive parents. His biological parents had been shipped off by the Germans in 1942, as part of a mass deportation of anyone not born on the island. They had been held in the castle at Bad Wurzach.

Naturally, Clive wanted to get back to the island as soon as possible to see his family and friends. But with the demands of post-war Germany – and even post-war Britain – calling, it would be some time before he could return home for good. When he did, he would have a family to support.

We worked hard to finish the bridge at Artlenburg, without thinking it could soon be all over. We never really thought about the end of the war, just of getting to the end of the day, the next time to eat, the next chance to sleep.

When the end of the war came, it didn't really end properly for us. We were outside a big barracks at Artlenburg, which was still full of Germans who were still fighting. We had to help clear them out with a lot of firing. Eventually they came out with their hands up. One of them was a Luftwaffe officer, who was making a big fuss about being captured, and getting a bit aggressive. I noticed he had an Iron Cross, and a nice ceremonial Luftwaffe dagger, so I told him in no uncertain terms who was boss, and got them both off him. I remembered how the Jerry had taken my watch when we were surrounded on the retreat to Dunkirk. Soon after that the war was over.

None of us was expecting that to happen, until suddenly the announcement was made. We had moved to a place called Neumünster, where we were billeted in a tannery. It bloody stank; it was a horrible place to be. But our major spread the news of the surrender around, and that cheered us all up. I think we might have had double food rations, and even a tot of rum.

Of course there was celebrating, but I also had a funny accident one time I went out for a drink with my mate – you always went out in twos. Anyway, we went into this bar, and everyone in there had sour faces because they had lost the war. We ordered a couple of beers, drank them, and went

In Germany, after the surrender.
I'm the handsome one on the right.

out. We were just walking up the street when I noticed a couple of nice-looking girls in short skirts on the other side. And you know what I was like for nice-looking girls! So there I was, eyeing them up, when bang! I walked straight into a concrete lamp post. I cut my face up around my eye really badly. The war was over, and this was probably my worst injury!

Not long after this, there was a notice put up on the board: 'Any Channel Islanders wanting to be part of the force to liberate and occupy the islands should put their names down here'. So of course I got my name down there bloody quick – and never heard any more about it. That was probably because I was so far up in Germany; it could have been too far to send me. I would have bloody loved to have been part of that. But I was really happy that Jersey was to be freed, and I could write to my friends and family again. But that took a lot of time, and apart from a short bit of compassionate leave we had to stay on in Germany as an army of occupation. And as engineers, our skills were always in demand: road repairs, bridge building, all the usual stuff. And the country had been so badly knocked about there was a lot to do!

I remember at Christmas-time, we were at a place called Neuenberg. They organised a Christmas dance for us, to cheer us all up. We hadn't had a nice dance for ages. The authorities decided they would invite a lot of the displaced persons, or DPs, from the area. Anyway, I had my eye on this nice-looking Jerry bird. So I invited her to the dance, and she said, 'Oh yes, I'd like to come!' She spoke better English than I did.

Anyway, we got to this dance and I was looking forward to it even though I've got two left feet. There I was, with my mates, showing off because we thought we were the big soldier boys. I said to them, 'Right, I'm going to have a dance with this German bird I've brought.' So I looked over to where she was standing with her friends, and whistled her over to the dance floor. And she came marching over to me and said, 'You whistle at dogs, not at young ladies!' and all my mates were laughing their bloody heads off.

We had to stay in Germany for a long time after peace was declared.

Because we were engineers, we were kept busy fixing bomb damage, roads and bridges. Of course I just wanted to get home.

Eventually I managed to get some compassionate leave. After I'd had a brief leave some months before, my wife was expecting our first child, and had managed to get back to Jersey soon after the Germans were kicked out.

I got called by the officers one morning and was told that my leave had been approved. I was taken to the Hook of Holland to get a boat, which took me to England. I can't remember which port we landed at, although it may have been Harwich. Then I can remember catching a train down to Southampton so I could get a boat across to Jersey. The one I took was quite small – smaller than a mail boat. All through my life, to and from Jersey, and across to invade France, I was never seasick. But on this boat they gave me a hammock to sleep in. I'd never used one before.

I slung it up in a small space – there wasn't much room. And the sea got pretty rough. The bloke in the hammock next to me was swinging this way and that as we hit the waves. Then I noticed another bloke in his hammock about five feet away from me. He was a petty officer in the navy. He looked up and I recognised him – he had been at school with me, and his name was Doug Clothier. I think he ended up as a bank manager. He recognised me too, so we said hello and shook hands. All the time the bloody boat was tossing up and down. He said, 'Why don't we go up on deck, and get some fresh air?' So up we went, and he went straight over to the rail, and *bleurggh*! 'Jesus Christ', I thought, 'a petty officer in the navy, seasick!' And that made me sick too! The first time in my life, and I'm set off by a sailor! He said he had been feeling ill down below, and reckoned it was the food he'd been given. We laughed about it afterwards. I was bringing a few things back, too. As well as the dagger and Iron Cross from the Luftwaffe officer, I'd managed to take revenge for the Jerry who took my watch off me on the retreat to Dunkirk; I had about thirty of them which I'd liberated from stroppy prisoners in my kit bag. I'd been into an abandoned house in Neumunster, and found a nice yellow glass decanter with glasses to go with it, which I managed to pack. I even had a Luger, a German pistol which everybody wanted to get hold of, they were very popular as souvenirs. But on the boat, they were warning us that we weren't allowed to take any firearms or ammunition ashore. I dropped it over the side.

Finally I got back to Jersey. I felt very proud of myself when I arrived: probably a bit big-headed. I was a soldier and I had done my bit. Everybody was patting me on the back, and I was quite well-known anyway, so lots of people talked to me.

Then my wife had our baby, and more battles began.

Generalfeldmarschall Wilhelm Keitel signs the
instrument of surrender in Berlin © IWM FRA 203385

German towns were badly damaged by the war.
We helped to re-open the roads and rebuild the bridges. © HU 44924

Map 1

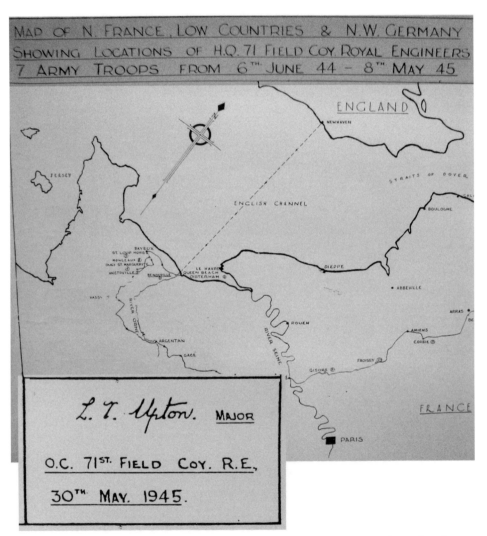

This is the map that our major produced and gave to each one of us after the war. He was known to the troops as Tiny as he was massive.

Map 2

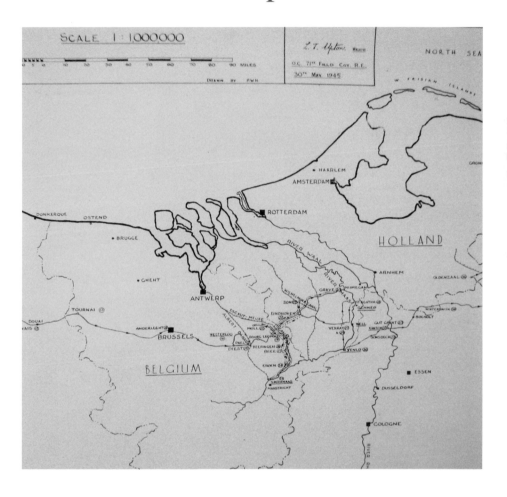

Map 3

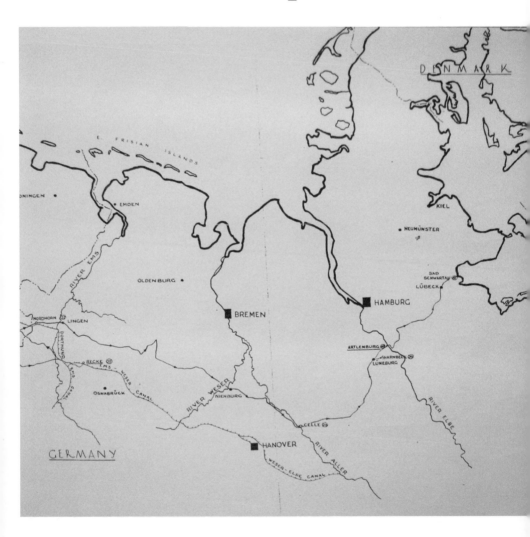

Close up detail

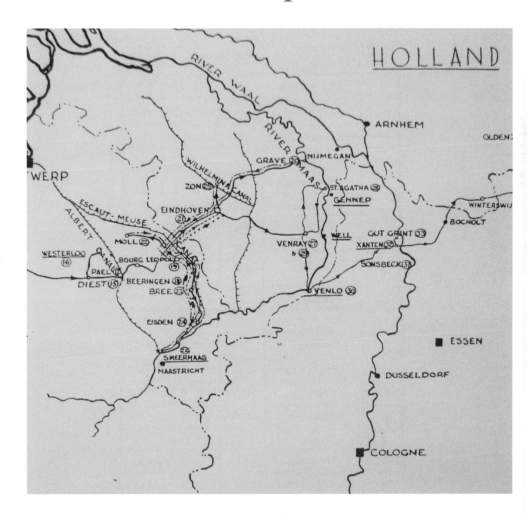

Location, distance and date details

SERIAL No.	PLACE NAME	DISTANCE IN MILES	DATE OF ARRIVAL AND DEPARTURE
1	OISTERHAM	O	6 JUNE 44.
2	BENOUVILLE	4	6 JUNE – 11 JULY
3	ST. LOUP HORS	26	11 JULY – 21 "
4	DUCY ST. MARGUERITE	34	21 " – 2 AUG
5	ANCTOVILLE	43	2 AUG – 9 "
6	MONCEAUX	54	9 " – 16 "
7	VASSY	85	17 " 23 "
8	VERNON	207	23 " 31 "
9	GISORS	229	31 " 1 SEPT.
10	FROISSY	258	1 SEPT. 2 "
11 & 12	CORBIE & BEARNAIS	328	SEPT. 2 – SEPT. 3
13	TOURNAI	366	" 3 – " 4
14	ANDERLECHT	416	" 4 – " 7
15	DIEST	451	" 7 – " 8
16	WESTERLOO	460	" 8 – " 13
17	PAEL	477	" 13 – " 16
18	BEERINGEN	479	" 17 – " 18
19	BOURG LEOPOLD	485	" 18 – " 21
20	GRAVE	543	" 21 – " 30
21	EINDHOVEN	573	" 30 – OCT.1

Location, distance and date details

SERIAL NO.	PLACE NAME	DISTANCE IN MILES	DATE OF ARRIVAL AND DEPARTURE
22	MOLL	601	OCT. 1 – OCT. 21
23	BREE	629	" 21 – NOV. 4
24	EISDEN	641	NOV.4 – NOV. 11
25	ZON	691	" 11 – DEC. 4
26	SMEERMAAS	753	DEC.4 – " 16
27	VENRAIJ	834	" 16 – FEB 11
28	ST. AGATHA	854	FEB 11 – MAR.1
29	VENRAIJ	874	MAR.1 – " 7
30	VENLO	890	" 7 – " 21
31	SONSBECK	911	" 21 – " 24
32	XANTEN	918	MAR.24 – MAR. 28
33	GUT GRINT	922	" 28 – APR. 6
34	WINTERSWIJK	955	APR.6 – " 10
35	RECKE	1,010	" 10 – " 13
36	OLDENZAAL	1,049	" 13 – " 14
37	NORDHORN	1,059	" 14 – " 23
38	CELLE	1,208	" 23 – " 24
39	SHARNBECK	1,270	" 24 – " 29
40	ARTLENBURG	1,285	" 29 – MAY 5
41	BAD SCHWARTAU	1,337	MAY 5 – " 8

Chapter Thirteen

HOME

The Jersey Clive was coming back to was very different from the Jersey he had left nearly six years before. It had suffered under the Occupation; ugly concrete bunkers, built by slaves and ringed with barbed wire and mines, blighted the beaches.

The people too had suffered, not only the indignity of subjugation to an enemy, but also hunger, cold and distrust. All had made their mark. Many islanders had been deported; some had died in the death camps.

Liberation had been a delirious time of celebration as the British forces landed and raised the Union Flag from the Pomme d'Or Hotel and the harbour master's office. But once the celebrations had died down, the islanders would have to get their lives back to normal. Some of those who had been deported came back to find their homes had been taken over by strangers, or looted for valuables, food or firewood.

German prisoners worked in gangs to repair the damage they had caused: to lift the mines and remove the barbed wire.

Of course there were the returning servicemen like Clive to look after too, although many men of service age had been trapped by the German invasion before they could join up.

Many islanders simply wanted to forget the war, and to get back to the lives they had been living before it began. Clive still finds it strange that they didn't seem to want to know about what had happened to him or the others who came back from the fighting.

He saw evidence of the Occupation all around him, but even now he finds it impossible to imagine Germans marching up the Parade or walking down King Street.

But as 1946 began, Clive had new battles to fight. His awful experiences in the war brought him nightmares from the past, while petty officialdom threatened his future.

My daughter was born at the Le Bas Centre. I was really pleased, because I'd wanted a little girl. I wasn't there for the actual birth, because they wouldn't let you in those days.

My wife was living with her parents in town. Her mum really liked me, but her dad didn't approve. He always slammed the door if I'd left it open, and made it clear he didn't like me.

Anyway, while I was there on leave, I went to the Housing Department to try and find us somewhere to live. I wore my best uniform, and saw a man called Major Hamilton. I think he was a First World War major, given a job by the States.

I knocked at the door and was invited to come in, so I went in and politely wished him a good morning. 'What do you want?' he asked, really bloody aggressive and unpleasant.

'Well sir,' I replied, 'I'm home on compassionate leave, my wife has just given birth to my daughter, and we are having to share this little house, and I was wondering if you could find us a States property?'

'How many children have you got then?' he asked me. I told him just the one. He looked up from the work he was doing – he was still writing something – and said, 'Well what I'd do if I was you is go back home and make another one. Then I might consider you.'

I wasn't happy at that! I said, 'I've been in the f***ing army since 1939, right through the war, I was at Dunkirk, on the beaches at D-Day, and that's how you treat me?' I told him the place stank, walked out and slammed the door behind me. We had to live with my in-laws for a while.

It worked out all right in the end, though. I was walking down Green Street towards the sea, where someone told me they had arranged some married quarters for soldiers who needed them. When I got there, I saw some German prisoners painting the walls of a building. I had my uniform on of course, so I went up to them and started chatting as soldiers. I still didn't dislike Germans really – only the Nazis who had started the whole thing. Anyway, we sort of chatted, with me trying to use some of the German I had learned while I was away. They managed to explain that I had to go to the building where the Territorial Army headquarters are now, to ask the major in charge about getting a place to live. So up I went, still fuming about the last major who hadn't helped me at all. The man I had to see was Major Le Brocq, who had been one of the liberating army who had landed in Jersey. I straightened myself up, knocked on the door, and heard him call me to come in. I marched in, and threw up a salute smartish, because he was there in uniform too. He asked me what I wanted, and I explained all the problems we'd had, including the rude response from housing.

'Well,' he said, 'I'd love to help you but there is quite a waiting list.'

'Here we go again,' I thought. I could see a long row of keys hanging on hooks just behind his desk, all waiting for lucky people to come and take for their new homes.

'Incidentally,' he said, 'what's your name?' I told him. 'Really?' he asked, 'Are you related to Basil Kemp?' I told him yes, that Percy Kemp was my biological father. 'Well, how about that!' he said. 'My sister has just married your brother Basil!' I hadn't known about this, because I'd been away, and I wasn't in very good contact with all my brothers and sisters anyway.

He looked at me with a smile, and gestured at the keys behind him. 'Take a few sets of keys,' he said, 'choose the flat you'd like, and let me have the rest back!' Well, I gave him the best salute I'd ever given anyone, and a big 'Thank you sir!'

I did have another problem though. I couldn't see my dad. My foster-brother, who was also called Basil, had got mixed up with a bad bunch just before the Occupation. He was ten years younger than me. He had pinched a German rifle, and the story is that he set fire to a hotel that the Germans were in, up at Bagatelle. Apparently, after the Germans left, somebody had grassed him up for having this rifle, and because he was a junior my foster-father had to go to court, and got sent to prison for six months.

I went to the Attorney General, whose offices were in Library Place. I went in my uniform, to try and impress him. I told him I had just come back from Germany, and that my dad was in prison because of what my brother had done. He said, 'The prison isn't a hotel you know. You can't just go in and visit when you like.' I said I'd been in the army, away in France and Germany, and hadn't seen him for six years. 'Very well,' he said, 'I'll let you go just this once!'

Above: The Germans who helped me find my new home. By coincidence this picture was in the local newspaper nearly seventy years later!
(Image courtesy of the Jersey Evening Post)

Left: Me and my foster-parents on my first leave after the end of the war

He gave me a visiting chit, and I headed off down Gloucester Street to the prison, where the hospital is now. I rang the bell, and a warder came to the gate. 'Yes,' he said, 'what do you want?' I said I had come to visit Mr Osborne. 'Oh, Charlie!' he said. 'He's painting somewhere. We've given him all the soft jobs.'

Then the prison governor came out. He shook my hand, and told me not to worry about my father. He had the freedom of the prison, and was painting the gates outside in Gloucester Street.

But what happened next was wonderful. There was a visit by the Home Secretary of the time, James Chuter Ede. He visited the prison, and was looking though the lists of prisoners and what they'd done. He asked about my father, and was told the story of the stolen rifle. He said people should have stolen more rifles from the Germans, and to let my father go!

Soon after this, I went to see Mum and Dad at their house. I found Dad with a black eye, and asked him what had happened. 'Oh, nothing, Son.' he said. But my mum told me it was my brother, who had become a right tearaway. He'd gone to Dad asking for money, and when he said no, he'd laid into him. Well, I went right up to his room and found him lying on the bed, drunk. I jumped right on top of him and gave him the bloody hiding of his life. From then on I had virtually nothing to do with him.

Mum and Dad told me a bit about what life had been like under the Occupation, and how they had fought to keep their lives as normal as possible. Apparently Mum had knocked a German down on her bike when he had stepped off the pavement, and she had been fined for that. Dad had told a soldier where to go when he came round asking for his laundry to be done. But apart from that they had had a relatively peaceful Occupation.

For me though, it really was an eventful leave. My biological father, Percy Kemp, was back in the island, running the Lion Hotel on the corner of Castle Street and Sand Street. My wife and I were walking through town one day, proud as punch with our new baby, when we bumped into my eldest sister. She made a right fuss of me, and the baby, because she hadn't seen me for ages. But then she said, 'I'm sure your father would love to see her!' I said no, but she insisted. She went into his pub and called the old bastard out. He came out, saw us with the baby, and jingled some coins in his pocket. 'Oh,' he said, 'she won't keep the family name up!'

'Thanks for that,' I said, and we went on our way. I did feel great being in uniform, though, going through town with my lovely wife and baby.

There were still quite a few Germans about, working to put the island straight again, but I didn't have any ill-feeling towards them. Of course I hadn't seen them in the island while they were in charge. I did, and still do, find it very hard to imagine them marching with their uniforms and guns up the Parade.

So the war was over; but it wasn't time for me to get back to a proper home life just yet. I had to wait to be demobbed. That meant going back to Germany for more work, while we waited for the army to decide it didn't want us any more.

Eventually I was sent to Halifax, where they were billeting soldiers waiting to get out of the army. My demob number was twenty-eight. But while I was there, the officer in charge found out that I was a gas fitter by trade. He went round the town trying to find us jobs to do, and I ended up working for the Halifax Gas Board. They were short of labour, and pleased to have me. They paired me up with this young Yorkshire lad, who showed me around, and I got him to carry my bags. They wanted me to stay there, and it was a good job, but I was a Jersey lad and had a wife and child there, so I wanted to go home. When my number came up, we were sent to this big mill in Halifax. 'Right,' the sergeant said, 'What's your size?' So I told him my size, and, typical army, he just bundled up this load of clothes and chucked it at me. I was given the choice of grey or blue pinstripes, and I got some that almost fitted. I think they gave me some shoes, and there was a choice of hats too. I think I got one that made me look like Spencer Tracy! They wanted my uniform back too, but I asked to keep it because I had to get all the way back to Jersey. They let me keep it, but I didn't manage to hang on to my greatcoat. That was a shame, because it was really special. I'd had pleats put into the back of it, and it looked really good with the collar up. When I was wearing it you'd believe that it was me, John Wayne and Errol Flynn who won the war! I don't think I ever wore the pinstripes; the jacket had huge shoulders and I didn't like it. I think I sold it.

I kept the uniform for a while, but eventually it was taking up too much space in the wardrobe so I got rid of it. Shame really, it was the same one which had taken me through France and Germany. I was always very good at looking after clothes, and always looked smart.

And that was it; I went straight home to Jersey.

The Jersey Gas Company was happy to have me back, and I got into a routine again. Even though some of the blokes there had been in the war, no one wanted to talk about it. I'd be walking around the shop floor, and no one would even ask me about it, no one wanted to know. If they had asked I would have told them, but it wasn't the done thing. The problem was, in Jersey especially, that people wanted to forget the war. They had been occupied, seen their friends and neighbours punished and sent away, and nobody wanted to think about that any more. They wanted to forget it, move on with their lives.

The only person who did want to know about it was my friend Dicky Maine, who was a historian. He always told me that if I hadn't joined the army, the war would have ended two years earlier! The two of us used to go on holiday to Europe together, looking for artefacts. He kept a little museum, with all the German gear on display.

Even my dad didn't really ask me about it. I came back with four medals, and he had only two from his time in the First War. But he always used to joke that his two were worth more than my four! I just remember him saying, 'I'm glad you're back, Son.'

There were always news films being shown at the cinema, all about the war and what had happened, but I never wanted to go. I'd seen enough of it, and didn't really want to be reminded. For months afterwards I'd have nightmares, waking up in a cold sweat in the middle of the night, re-living some of the terrible things I'd seen. It took a long time to get them out of my head, and even now a lot of them are still so fresh it seems like yesterday.

One thing that did help me was the fact that we had very little money. That meant I was always busy, trying to make ends meet for our little family. The flat we'd chosen in the married quarters was at the end of the block, close to the sea, and really clean and tidy, even if it was a bit small. I'd go to work at the Gas Company first thing in the morning, and put in a full day with the tools, fitting and fixing people's boilers and cookers. Then I'd be straight down the docks to see if there was any work there, loading potatoes or taking stuff to ships from the warehouses there. By the time I got home I'd be knackered, but there was always the allotment to sort out too. Just behind the married quarters, where the flats are now, there were allotments going up the hill towards Fort Regent. Ours was towards the top, and you had to get a ladder to get to most of it, because the spaces were cut into the side of the hill like steps. I used to grow stuff there to help to feed the family. Lots of spuds, lettuce, peas and beans. My army discipline helped a lot; my allotment was always tidy, and I always kept it watered no matter how tired I was. If I had a good crop, I'd bag it up and take it down to the market, where I could sell a lot of it to the stallholders there.

The hardest part was getting the wraic up there, to put on the potatoes. I'd be down on the beach after a hard day's work, with a fork and a wheelbarrow, collecting the stuff. Then I'd push it back up the hill to the bottom of the ladder, then have to carry it up by the bag. It was worth it though; it kept us fed and gave us some extra money too. Another old bloke who lived there let me have his allotment, so I had more room to grow – but more work too.

That was how my life as a civilian began. It was very hard, and we had to work like hell to make ends meet. But it was good to be home.

Chapter Fourteen

MOVING ON

Clive had been successful in the Jersey Gas Company before he left to go to war, and it seemed only natural for him to go back there. He had always had a very strong work ethic; from the age of fourteen he did his job with pride and was always very smart. As he worked his way up, he made sure he had a wardrobe full of suits and shirts so he was always presentable.

That didn't mean that he wanted to rise above the other men though. Clive always considered himself 'one of the blokes', and never tried to set himself above the rest of the workers who picked up their bags of tools each day. As his wartime experiences showed, he was never comfortable with authority!

Eventually his skills and organisation singled him out for promotion, which he reluctantly took, and he gained more and more authority until he finally retired as a supervisor in 1985.

The work that he did, travelling around the island installing and checking gas appliances, has left him with a great knowledge of Jersey. Mention any street, anywhere, and he will be able to tell you, 'Ah yes, I put the boilers in that estate ...'

It was long after he had retired that Clive finally had the chance to re-live what had happened during the war.

Because I was a hard worker, I started to make my way in the Gas Company. My work was always good; I was reliable, and happy to work extra hours.

Eventually, the boss said I should go and get my City and Guilds exams so that I could climb up the ladder. He told me it would help me a lot.

I had to go two nights a week, learning some theory and some practical. The problem was, I was happy doing what I was doing, working with tools, and I really didn't want to step up to be a manager.

I told them I didn't want to change, and wanted to stay as I was, working as a fitter. But one day I drove the van back into work at about half past five, and there was a foreman waiting for me. He said, 'Clive, Wedgie wants you.' Wedgie was our name for the boss, Mr Wedgewood.

Well, if Wedgie wanted you, it was usually for a bollocking. I wondered if someone was complaining that I sometimes went for a cup of tea and a bacon roll in a café in the market before I started work. In fact, a few days before, there was a woman there who thought that me and my mates had been laughing at her, and I wondered if she had been in to moan about it. We hadn't been laughing at her, but even so, it had me worried.

Wedgie had a proper old-fashioned office. You rang a bell outside, and there was a sign which would say either 'wait' or 'enter'. So I washed my hands and went up there, and rang the bell. My hands were shaking. In those days, you were afraid of the boss.

'Enter' said the sign, so in I went. There he was, on the other side of this bloody great desk, and I was shaking more and more. 'OK Clive,' he said, 'Sit down.'

Now the fact that he called me Clive and asked me to sit down meant it wasn't a bollocking, so I relaxed. But he still had a bit of a go at me. 'Mr Tucker has tried to get you to do your City and Guilds,' he said, 'and now he has retired, and so has Mr Walters.' These were blokes who were the next level above me, managers of the working men. 'What I'm trying to tell you,' he said, 'is that your work is really top quality, better than any of the other fitters. We've been watching you. Your time sheets are immaculate, with careful notes, everything is very good. We want you to be a supervisor now, and have some responsibility.'

I told him I didn't want to do that, that I was happy with the tools.

'You might be happy with the tools,' he said, 'but from this minute you're a supervisor.'

I thought about it, and asked if I could go home and speak to my wife about it.

'You can speak to Jesus Christ about it if you like,' he said, 'you're a supervisor. We aren't happy about the supervisors we have, and we want you to do the job. And I'll tell you something else. You're younger than most of the fitters, and they will try to make trouble for you. So I want to make things better by giving you five years' back pay if you take the job.' And that was a hell of a lot of money! So I became a supervisor, and only had one bit of trouble. This bloke came up to me and poked me in the chest. He said, 'If you think I'm taking orders from you, you've got another thing coming!'

'Don't tell me that,' I replied, 'go and tell Mr Wedgewood, he gave me the job and I didn't ask for it.'

He came around eventually, and apologised to me. I made a good foreman in the end. I tidied up the office, and arranged a booking system for all the jobs which kept a record of what everyone did. I had about sixty men under me.

We had some trouble when we changed from coal gas to liquid gas. It meant lots of work had to be done to convert people's appliances, and they brought in a load of cowboys from England to do it. I was on the phone all the time, trying to sort out problems. Some of these blokes seemed to do sweet FA all the way through the job, and then claimed overtime too. I had to work so hard to try and keep everything on track, to make sure everyone got their jobs done, and hardly had any time to relax. Eventually, when it was all done, the boss got us all together to thank us. Then he asked me up to his office to thank me properly, and I thought I might do quite well out of it. In the end, he gave me this little

155

food parcel, worth about a fiver! I said, 'Thanks, sir, but I don't really need it, just give it to charity!' Some of the blokes working on that job had made enough money to buy houses, and here's me with a fiver's-worth of food for my trouble! Thing is, I was always honest and never claimed for work that I hadn't done.

So I settled into a steady life. I brought up my family, and slowly the memories of the war faded. My nightmares faded away. In the end, I stayed at the gasworks for the rest of my working life. I kept myself very busy, running about at work and with all my different hobbies.

But there was one very sad time; when my wife Doreen, who I had met and married during the war, died.

She was only fifty-six, and became very ill with cancer. I stayed at home to look after her, but of course I had to keep my job too. I arranged to have some people come in to help out, and Mary was one of those who volunteered. She was married to one of my brothers, but going through a divorce. She and I got on so well that a year or so after Doreen died, we married. I've been with her ever since, and count myself very lucky to have had two wonderful wives in my life.

As I came near retirement, I was told I needed to go to the States housing department every six months to tell them what I was doing, and make sure my name was down for a nice place to live. We'd been living in company housing all the time I'd been working. So every six months, religiously, we'd go there and remind them we were hoping for somewhere to go.

The final time, when I had actually retired, this woman at housing looked through my records. 'Right,' she said. 'I've been looking at your records. You've got a pension from the Gas Company, and your old age pension too. And I see you were in the army, so you'll get an army pension. I'm sorry, but we can't consider you for a States home.'

Well, Mary was crying by the time we got out of there, and I was very angry. Luckily, the company didn't want to throw us out right away, so we had time to find a new place. Eventually we found somewhere at First Tower where we had to pay hundreds of pounds a week in rent.

50 years with Jersey Gas

FIFTY years service with the Jersey Gas Company was marked yesterday when Mr Clive Kemp was presented with gifts from the board to recognise his long period of employment.

Mr Kemp (64), who lives with his wife Mary at their home in

CATHY LE FEUVRE reports

St Saviour's Road, joined the Gas Company on December 15, 1934, as an apprentice fitter. He completed his apprenticeship in 1939, and on the outbreak of war volunteered to serve with

the Royal Engineers.

Posted to France with the British Expeditionary Forces in April, 1940, barely two months after his enlistment, Mr Kemp took part in the evacuation of Dunkirk on June 1 that year.

He remained in England and was attached to a bomb disposal unit throughout the Blitz, and he also took part in the D-Day landings in Normandy with an assault bridging unit.

On his demobilisation in 1946, Mr Kemp returned to the Island and rejoined the Gas Company as a fitter, and in 1971 was promoted to district inspector. Seven years later he was made a base inspector, a position which he still holds. He is due to retire at the end of the year.

Sporting links

In the past Mr Kemp has had strong links with local sporting bodies, his principal interests being football and athletics, and he has represented the company's sports club on numerous occasions.

Mr Kemp has also been secretary of the Saturday Football League, assistant secretary of the Jersey Football Association and founder president of the now defunct Jersey Scooter Club.

He now lives a much quieter life, and his main enjoyment is music and hi-fi.

Mr Kemp has one stepdaughter and four grandchildren, and his stepfather, Mr Charlie Osborne, a the age of 94, is still a pensioner of the Jersey Gas Company.

Mr Clive Kemp: From Jersey Gas to Dunkirk and back again

(Image courtesy of the Jersey Evening Post)

157

After all I'd gone through, that was how they treated us. I'm not a bitter bloke, but it rankles with me still, it really does.

I finally retired in 1985, after fifty-one years on the company books. They included my army time in that too, and the times I'd been liable for call-up.

Being retired meant I could get back into one of my earlier hobbies. I'd been pretty good at snooker before the war, and had been in the first division at the age of eighteen. The war put a stop to my playing for years, and when I got back to Jersey I was too busy. I was the sort of bloke who would stay at home with his family in the evenings, never one for going down the pub.

But when I retired I went out and bought a cue again, and got right back into it. I joined the Mechanics Club, and played as often as I could, sometimes every morning. I never got to be quite as good as I had been when I was a young man, but I was the over-sixties club champion. I was always able to hold my own against anyone. The youngsters, with their good eyesight, would play a potting game, while I was better at the defensive, snookering tactics. Today, when I watch it on television, I can predict which shots the professionals will take.

I played golf for a while too. Me and three mates used to go down to the course for lessons, but I never took it too seriously. I was always messing about. When you hit a perfect shot though, there's a wonderful ping which tells you it's gone just right. And it's the same with snooker when you hit the cue ball on the sweet spot. I was always a competitive player, always playing to win. Sometimes I would put people off because I wanted to do well.

The other sport I am a big fan of is football. I played that until I was forty. Every year there would be a real needle match, between the Gas Company and the Electricity Board. It really was a grudge match, with people kicking each other all over the pitch. And in those days, you wore boots with steel toecaps, so they really hurt. I lost my two front teeth in the last match I ever played, when someone went for the ball, which was in the air. They missed, and caught me in the face instead. I was quite a lazy footballer though. If there were eleven blokes wanting to play, I'd always volunteer to be the reserve or the linesman.

Then one day I went to a meeting with the Saturday Football League, as a delegate for the company. It was a big league, running about twenty matches every weekend. The meeting took place at 16 New Street – that building has since been re-opened as a National Trust property because of its history. During the meeting I somehow got chosen to help out as an assistant secretary. All of the players had to be listed, with details if they had scored or been given a disciplinary warning which made them ineligible to play. I did that for about eight years, and then became secretary. I ran it for another six years or so, and then became assistant secretary of the Jersey Football Association. That gave me quite a few perks, like being able to get Cup Final tickets.

Me with the great Stanley Matthews when he visited Jersey

Since I had more free time when my daughter had grown up, I could spend more of it enjoying myself. When I wasn't playing football or snooker, I spent a lot of time on my scooter. Boudin's in town was the place where me and my mates would buy our Lambrettas, and I became president of the Jersey Scooter Club. That was a big job too, planning outings for every weekend. We called ourselves the Harlequins, because all of our scooters were different colours.

With the help of my family, and all my hobbies, I gradually forgot about the war. Until one day I saw an advert in the paper.

My surprise ninetieth birthday cake made as a snooker table.
That is me made out of marzipan.

160

Chapter Fifteen

VETERAN

When the war ended, nearly all of the men who had been called up to fight were demobbed. They left their comrades, the brothers in arms with whom they had served, and went back to Civvy Street. Once there, they got on with their lives as best they could, in austere times still governed by rationing and the need to change from a wartime economy to a peacetime one.

Few of the returned soldiers, sailors or airmen wanted to dwell on what they had seen; and it seemed few wanted to listen to them. Clive's experience was typical; he had little wartime experience in common with his work colleagues, and his former comrades lived a long way away, so the war was simply forgotten about.

But times change. As a new generation which hadn't experienced wartime grew up, they started to ask questions, and interest started to grow again. The old soldiers who had served in the war began to talk about their experiences. They in turn began to talk more to each other, and veterans associations grew across the country.

The first branch of the Normandy Veterans Association was formed in Grimsby in 1981, and more were set up as men in towns all over Britain answered advertisements in their local papers. After all the years of silence, many of them relished the chance to talk about what had happened to them with others who had shared similar experiences.

Clive saw an advertisement in the *Jersey Evening Post* in 1995, and went along to see what would happen. It would be the beginning of a new chapter in his life, and he quickly became an important member of the group.

After all those years of silence, Clive could now tell his story to people who wanted to listen. Interest grew quickly, and he made regular visits to local schools, together with former Para Sid Peck, to talk about the war. He appeared in the local paper, and was a special guest at the opening of the new museum at Pegasus Bridge. Eventually his story came to the attention of some very important people, and he was awarded the *Légion d'honneur* – France's highest decoration. Typically, he maintains that it was not just for him, but shared by all of the Jersey Normandy Veterans Association.

The advert had been taken out by a very nice chap called Dick Connew. He was an Englishman who had served on RAF rescue boats during the war. It asked if any veterans of the Normandy campaign would like to meet at the Société Jersiaise in Pier Road. About thirty of us turned up, and there was a photo of us all in the paper, standing on the steps there.

Our first meeting, which local historian Michael Ginns helped to organise

We all talked, and for many of us it was the first time we had spoken about the war. It was as though there had been an unwritten law, that we would keep it to ourselves. It brought things out that we had kept quiet about for a long time. A lot of the time we talked about the funny things which had happened to us during the war. We didn't want to remember the awful things right away.

Bill Reynolds in particular was a very interesting person to chat to, because he had been in the same areas as me, because he was in supplies. Eventually though, when we all got to know each other, we stopped talking about it again. We just became friends.

We eventually decided that there were enough of us to make an association. Dick and I got on very well, and worked out how to make it happen. Dick was the president, and Peter Manton was the secretary at first, until I took over.

We began to have regular meetings, and then dinners where we could bring our wives and families. Even so, the talk now isn't often about the war.

People's perceptions of it seem to have changed over the years. At first, immediately afterwards, it seemed no one wanted to know. I kept quiet about what I'd seen and done, and nobody asked me about it. But in more recent years, people have become much more interested. When I was young it had only just happened, but now it's history.

When the film *Saving Private Ryan* came out, the newspaper asked us all to go to watch it and then talk about it afterwards.

I can't say I enjoyed it, because it was very American, the usual Yankee over the top stuff. It did show people what happened though; the dead men floating in the water, the noise of the guns and the bombs. That took me right back.

The article in the paper put us in the public eye a bit; for many of us it was the first time people had heard about what we'd done. People were coming up to us and calling us heroes, and I've never been very comfortable with that. I'm not a bloody hero. The boys that we left behind us, the ones who didn't come back, they were the heroes. Don't get me wrong, I'm proud of what I did, but I'm no hero.

Because of the exposure we were getting, more people were contacting me to hear my story. The people who run the new museum at Bénouville, the Pegasus Memorial, got in touch with me. They wanted to rebuild the original Pegasus Bridge right next to the new one, on the museum site. They invited me to come and officially open it, and there's a photo of me standing next to it in the official museum guidebook.

D-Day marchpast in Normandy. I am centre front.

Then there was the sixtieth anniversary of D-Day, which was a huge celebration. Veterans from all over the world came to Normandy. There were American marines, Canadian commandos, soldiers, sailors and airmen from every country you can think of. The prime minister and the US president were there too for the big ceremonies. We went over from Jersey and got on a big coach which took us to the beaches, but we were really just mixed in with the crowds.

My mate Fred and I were going to be special guests at the biggest event in Arromanches. We were told we had to be at a certain place at two o'clock to be picked up; so there we were, bang on time. Eventually the coach arrived, and took us up to the cliffs above Arromanches, where all the dignitaries were, ready to pin medals on us all. President Mitterand was pinning them on as people's names were called. But he only got round to doing the officers, and us other ranks got bugger all! At least we got to take part in the marchpast, though, something I'll never forget: hundreds of us with our flags under the sunshine all with

165

At George Dransfield's grave. It could have been mine. A friend I will never forget.

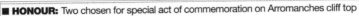

Jersey veterans to join
the Queen on D-Day

D-Day Heroes
Islanders who helped to liberate Europe

BY PAULA THELWELL

TWO of Jersey's D-Day veterans will be attending the main international commemoration of the Normandy Landings on 6 June.

Just ten British veterans have been invited to join the Queen, Prime Minister Tony Blair, President George W Bush and other head of states at the Arromanches cliff top homage on 6 June, and Fred Newton and Clive Kemp will be among the select band.

Mr Newton (79), the vice-chairman and youngest member of the Jersey Normandy Veterans Association Branch 100, said it was a great honour.

'We are representing fallen comrades covering all the services and that makes it very special, absolutely very special and I don't deserve it,' he said.

Mr Newton said the original plan was for each country to have 100 veterans present at the ceremony but since preparations began two years ago that had been whittled down to 50 and now just ten.

Mr Kemp (83), whose war record includes being evacuated from Dunkirk, helping dispose of unexploded bombs during the Blitz, and surviving Operation Market Garden, as well as D-Day, was also delighted to be among the few.

'I feel rather humbled and very honoured and I'm looking forward to it.'

The two men, and the other 14 Jersey veterans travelling to France for the 60th, and last official, commemoration of D-Day, face a busy weekend.

They leave Jersey on Saturday 5 June and attend the first event, the opening of the British Peace Garden by Prince Charles at the Caen Memorial Museum, at 5 pm.

On D-Day itself the Jersey party will attend the main British commemoration at the British Military Cemetery in Bayeux, which will be led by the Queen and the Prime Minister Tony Blair. They will also take part in a march past at Arromanches that evening.

● **D-Day Heroes: Page 21**

Clive Kemp and Fred Newton are two of only ten veterans invited to join heads of state in a special ceremony on 6 June

(Image courtesy of the Jersey Evening Post)

A very memorable day at Buckingham Palace

To Pegasus Bridge
with our veterans

With the band of Jersey. I am in the middle. (Image courtesy of the Jersey Evening Post)

When I was 82 I had five flying lessons over the D-Day beaches. Here's Pegasus Bridge. The bridge we built would be at the bottom left of this photo.

our medals on. That will always stay in my mind.

Afterwards though, it all went wrong. The organisers told us to wait at the top of the hill above the town, so we could be picked up and taken back to our hotel. We were there, we waited, and waited, and no one came for us. Eventually we walked all the way down the hill into Arromanches but we couldn't find any transport at all. So we walked all the way back up again, in the bloody hot sun, and waited at the top of the bloody hill with only an apple to eat! There was no one else about. In the end, a jeep with a couple of redcaps turned up and they asked what we were doing there.

We told them what had happened, that nobody had come to pick us up, and we hadn't even got a bloody medal! 'Right!' they said, 'Get in, we'll take you back!' and they took us all the way back to our hotel. It was the first time in my life I'd been glad to see a military policeman!

Later that trip we went to Pegasus Bridge, and there were loads of young soldiers there, many of them engineers. They all wanted to meet me, to shake my hand and ask me what it was like. It made me so proud that they would want to know me, and I swelled up as they asked me all the questions and wanted photos. They said I must have been really scared, and I said, 'No – I only shit myself twice ...!'

Of course when I'm there I always have to go and visit the Café Gondrée and meet Arlette, the lady who was a little girl when I was there on D-Day.

The Association continued for several years, and then one day I had a letter through the post, telling me I was to be awarded the *Légion d'honneur*! That's a very high medal in France – very few people get that. It was for all the work I'd done in setting up the Veterans Association, keeping it all together, organising all the trips and things. It was a bit of a shock, to be honest. Another member, Fred Newton, was to get one too, for his work organising our first trip.

Originally we were due to get them when we were in Normandy at the big anniversary, but that hadn't happened. So we waited and waited, until another letter arrived telling us we'd have to go to Germany for them; then another one delaying it again!

Myself and Sid Peck with some modern-day soldiers at Pegasus
Bridge – giving them the old bullshit!

Eventually we went to the French Embassy in London, to be presented with the medal by a French admiral. You see, you can only be given the medal of the *Légion d'honneur* by someone who already has it. It was an honour to meet all the other people there. It was such a posh place, you wondered if you should take your shoes off before you walked on the carpet. All the furnishings, the chairs and things, were so plush, it was like another world. Unfortunately we'd missed the food! I was feeling quite nervous because of all the splendour there, and the high ranking people all round me. Now I always start to make jokes when I'm nervous. When this admiral came down the line and reached me, and he pinned the medal on me, he leaned forward to kiss me, as they do in France. 'No tongues!' I said. He was very nice, a very high ranking man, but he said he was really pleased to meet someone who had done the things I had done.

170

Being presented with the the Légion d'honneur. No tongues!

The next time I was in France, at the Café Gondrée, Madame Gondrée greeted me and looked for my medals. I wasn't wearing them – I'd left them in the coach. 'Well go and put them on!' she said, 'You are a *Légion d'honneur*!' It's a big deal over there. She wanted to show everyone my medals, and tell them who I was.

Soon after that we had an invitation for our branch of the veterans to go to a garden party at Buckingham Palace. We all went, and it was a real eye-opener. To get into the palace itself is an honour. As we walked in through the archway, my eyes were everywhere. There was this huge courtyard, and all around it were gas lamps, proper old ones, with a little chain to put them on and off, which were still lit! Now gas lamps, as I knew well, really are a thing of the past. You wouldn't expect to see them in Buckingham Palace.

Then we were ushered up these wide, carpeted stairs, through this room with beautiful cabinets all around it, to the gardens at the back. They were huge, and all along the back there were canopies with loads of food and drink; you could have fed a thousand people. It was a lovely day, and I was just standing there looking around. There were a few celebrities I noticed, but I tried to ignore them. Then I looked about thirty yards away to one side, and I noticed this lady, chatting to a couple of very high ranking officers. I thought, 'I know her face from somewhere.' But I couldn't see her properly because she had a big hat on. I thought, 'Who would I know at Buckingham Palace!' and tried to get on with talking to my mates. All of a sudden I heard my name called out, 'Clive!' It was that lady, and I realised then why I knew her; it was Madame Gondrée! So I put my drink down and went over to her. She introduced me to the two generals she had been talking to, the two leaders of the British Army at the time. She told them all about me, how I'd landed on D-Day, and helped build the bridge near her parents' café. They said they were really pleased to meet me, and wanted to shake my hand. One of them started asking about my medals, because he could see I had quite a few. 'What are those two?' he asked me. 'Well,' I said, 'that's the Dunkirk medal ...' and before I could say anything else, Madame Gondrée jumped in and said, 'And that's the *Légion d'honneur!*'

With Arlette Gondrée – old friends together again

We chatted a while, then I had to get back to my mates. But first I asked one of the generals if he would take my picture with Madame. He was happy to, so I pulled out my little tuppenny ha'penny camera, set it, and gave it to him. The next time we went to France, I gave her a framed copy of it.

I always watch the Remembrance Service from Whitehall on the television with tears in my eyes, because it brings so much back. And in Jersey, when they have D-Day or Armistice Day memorials, I'm often asked to read the Kohima Epitaph. 'When you go home, tell them of us and say, for your tomorrow, we gave our today.' But often I can't finish it, and the words stick in my throat. It all comes back. I see the television coverage of dead soldiers coming back from Iraq and Afghanistan, wrapped in flags with a big parade, and remember all of the mates I buried in a blanket in a field.

I'm a proud veteran. I volunteered. I did my bit. And if it happened again now, and they asked me, I would do it again.

Did you really win the war all by yourself Papa?

With my grandsons Jayden and Myles. They are the reason I told my story and I hope one day they will understand what really happened.

Me with the love of my life, Mary. Taken at the French Embassy
when I was presented with the Légion d'honneur.

EPILOGUE

I've been very lucky in my life. I had many happy years with my first wife, Doreen, and now Mary and we have been together since 1980. We have two young grandsons, and couldn't be happier. I'm twenty-four years older than Mary, but age doesn't matter if you love each other – and we do!

Walking is difficult for me now without my frame, as I have lost all the feeling in my feet. But my family and friends keep me going strong, and I haven't lost my sense of humour – or any of my marbles!

I'm in my ninety-fourth year now, and have a lifetime of memories, mostly happy. Sharing them with Chris over the past two years has been a wonderful experience, and I have come to look upon him as the son I never had.

Some people call me a hero. But I'm not. I'm just an ordinary fellow who has had a very lucky life.